CHOOSING CRIME

CHOOSING CRIME
The Criminal Calculus of Property Offenders

Kenneth D. Tunnell
Eastern Kentucky University

Nelson-Hall Publishers/Chicago

Project Editor: Rachel Schick
Cover Design: Corasue Nicholas
Cover Painting: *Timmy's Place* by Paul Madalinski

"Bob Dylan's Blues" (Bob Dylan) © 1963 Warner Bros. Inc.
All Rights Reserved. Used by permission.

"I Just Got Tired of Being Poor" Written by Dallas Frazier. © 1969 Acuff-Rose Music, Inc. (BMI) Used by permission / International copyright secured / All Rights Reserved.

"Nebraska" and "Meeting across the River" used by permission of The Bruce Springsteen Company.

Library of Congress Cataloging-in-Publication Data

Tunnell, Kenneth D.
    Choosing crime : the criminal calculus of property offenders / Kenneth D. Tunnell.
    p.   cm.
    Includes bibliographical references and index.
    ISBN 0-8304-1242-5
    1. Larceny—Tennessee—Public opinion. 2. Thieves—Tennessee—Attitudes. 3. Prisoners—Tennessee—Attitudes. 4. Crime—Tennessee—Decision making—Case studies. 5. Public opinion—Tennessee. I. Title.
HV6651.T86   1992
364.1'6'09768—dc20   91-29048
                                                                                                    CIP

Copyright © 1992 by Kenneth Tunnell

All rights reserved. No part of this book may be reproduced in any form without permission in writing from the publisher, except by a reviewer who wishes to quote brief passages in connection with a review written for broadcast or for inclusion in a magazine or newspaper. For information address Nelson-Hall Inc., Publishers, 111 North Canal Street, Chicago, Illinois 60606.

Manufactured in the United States of America

10 9 8 7 6 5 4 3 2 1

The paper used in this book meets the minimum requirements of American National Standard for Information Sciences—Permanence of Paper for Printed Library Materials, ANSI Z39.48-1984.

This book is dedicated to a wonderful, loving, and supportive family—my dad and sisters, and my mother, who would have danced a jig if she could have seen this work in print.

Contents

Acknowledgments	ix
1 Choosing Crime: A Theoretical and Empirical Orientation	1
2 Methods and Procedures	13
3 The Motivation to Commit Property Crime	37
4 Alternatives to Crime Commission	55
5 Neutralizing Fears During Criminal Decision Making	73
6 Let's Do It: Deciding to Commit a Crime	85
7 Whoa Now: Deciding Not to Commit a Crime	103
8 A Taxonomy of Criminal Decision Making	113
9 Conclusion: What Shall Be Done?	159
References	175

Acknowledgments

While at the University of Tennessee, a colleague of mine, Chris Link, and I learned that the National Institute of Justice (NIJ) intended to financially support qualitative research on repetitive property criminals. During the next few weeks, Chris and I developed a research proposal. Then, along with Neal Shover, we revised and submitted the proposal to NIJ and were fortunate enough to receive funding for our project.[1] Before the project got off the ground, Chris left the university. But to him, I owe a word of thanks for developing with me the original research proposal, for being a very supportive colleague, and above all, a good friend.

David Honaker, who entered the project after Chris's leaving, and I developed the research agenda, the topical interview guides, and collected and analyzed the data. David and I traveled throughout most of Tennessee, where we not only interviewed the participants but also related to each other what we had learned during the interviews. Those "thinking aloud" sessions, which took place over hundreds of miles of highway, proved very fruitful for making sense of the qualitative data and grappling with the elusive conclusions. I thank David for talking through with me the different stories we heard from the participants.

Neal Shover, who directed the study, taught me the subtle nuances of qualitative research strategies and how to manage and make sense of the data. I thank Neal for teaching by example.

Jim Black at the University of Tennessee was especially helpful by his willingness to give me some added direction and for getting some early data analysis back on track. Mike Benson offered invaluable feedback during the study and has offered support and encouragement for my work since that time. Don Clelland not only provided very critical and constructive comments about the study, but also taught me more than he may ever realize. He is a gifted, committed, and kind teacher and scholar.

Bob Gorman at the University of Tennessee first suggested the idea of putting this study into book form. He offered well-informed logistical advice on how to get this book off the ground and has continually shown interest in this work as it has progressed. Bob is, above all else, a true friend.

My department chairman, Larry Gaines, and my colleagues at Eastern Kentucky University have been very encouraging as I have labored over this manuscript.

My mate, Ilona Leki, has offered well-thought-out advice and invaluable commentary, and has encouraged me with her loving support and her joyous comradery. Thank you, Ilona, for everything.

The kind folks at Nelson-Hall, especially Richard Meade and Rachel Schick, have made this a truly exciting and rewarding experience. I greatly appreciate their support and diligence.

I thank the sixty men who willingly talked and shared with me their decision-making processes. This study would not have been possible without them and their cooperation. I also thank the Tennessee Department of Corrections for their cooperation in conducting this research.

NOTE

1. This project was funded by the National Institute of Justice (Grant #86-NIJ-CX0068). The interpretations in this work are those of the author and do not necessarily represent the official positions or policies of the National Institute of Justice.

Choosing Crime: A Theoretical and Empirical Orientation

Introduction

Crime is a very real concern to most Americans. Although seemingly random violent crimes appear to be those of gravest concern to the public, property crime constitutes 90 to 95 percent of all known crimes (Wright, 1985). Recent statistics show that most American adults have either been the victim of a property crime or know someone who has been[1] (Flanagan and Jamieson, 1988). The lost-dollar amount in stolen goods and the frequency at which property crimes are committed in this country are indeed alarming. The most recent national data inform us that a property crime occurs every three seconds and in 1989 over thirteen billion dollars worth of property was stolen (Bureau of Justice, 1990a). This staggering amount of stolen property and the frequency of property crime commission would lead the uninformed reader to assume that behind every bush and under every rock, criminals readily await their victims, that crime is qualitatively and quantitatively worse today than at any other time in our history, and that one's chances of being victimized are extremely high. But, this may not necessarily be the case.[2]

In the past few years, we have learned that the majority of property crimes are committed by a relatively small proportion of repeat offenders, sometimes labeled "career criminals" (Greenwood, 1982; Blumstein, 1986). One early study on the pervasiveness of criminal involvement found that among 624 criminals, 25 percent had committed 60 percent of all the sample's armed robberies and burglaries (Peterson et al., 1980). This group and others like it are labeled "problem populations," because during their "careers" in crime, they are responsible for committing a disproportionate number of thefts, burglaries, armed robberies, forgeries, and dealings in stolen goods. These repeat offenders are believed to function within a "criminal career" characterized by the "longitudinal sequence of crimes committed by an individual offender" (Blumstein et al., 1986: 12). Such a criminal career, some researchers believe, is much like the way a legitimate career represents a life-long commitment, for the primary components of a criminal career—participation, frequency, duration, and seriousness—are not unlike the components of a legitimate career (e.g., Walters, 1990).

The organization and structure of criminal careers and networks has received considerable attention among academics (Shover, 1972, 1973; Best and Luckenbill, 1982). Prior to that attention, a number of case studies of individual offenders were published. Such studies illuminate the logistics of crime, criminal networks, criminal ideologies about legitimate work, the lure of crime, and the autonomy that a criminal lifestyle affords (Sutherland, 1937; Chambliss, 1972; Inciardi, 1977). Case studies of repetitive criminals indicate that individuals enter this alternative profession early in life and learn the trade much in the same manner as those who enter legitimate professions (Sutherland, 1937; Irwin, 1970; Chambliss, 1972; Letkemann, 1973; Inciardi, 1977; Farrington, 1979; Luckenbill, 1985).

Repetitive criminals typically begin their careers in crime in their youth and often terminate them only with impending old age (Irwin, 1970; Frazier, 1976; Meisenhelder, 1977; Greenberg, 1983; Hirschi and Gottfredson, 1983; Shover, 1985). However, due primarily to methodological limitations of previous studies, little is known about the *nature* and *incidence* of their offending (Buckle and Farrington, 1984), how they decide to commit crimes, and how threats of punishment fit into their criminal calculus.[3] As recent researchers critically commented, "the question has not properly been considered whether those individuals who habitually make criminal decisions think in different ways from other people" (Clarke and Cornish, 1985: 161).

Although repetitive criminals typically are formally punished at some point in their lives, their criminal involvement continues even after they experience various sanctions. They may be arrested, jailed or imprisoned numerous times but they are not often dissuaded by their personal experiences with formal punishment. In fact, a recent government study indicates that official state punishment deters few criminals who are committed to crime and that 80 percent of the people held in local jails had a prior criminal conviction, two-thirds had served time before in a jail or prison, and about a third had served at least two prior sentences (Bureau of Justice Statistics, 1986). Since, after their release, 49 percent of former prisoners return to prison again, they apparently are little persuaded to desist from crime (Beck and Shipley, 1987). How repetitive criminals incorporate their experiences with punishment and the threat of future punishment into their decisions to continue committing crimes is, at this time, unclear.

Given our limited knowledge of the nature and incidence of committing crimes repeatedly and how the process of evaluating punishment threats fits within the criminal calculus, this research was designed to study how repetitive property offenders decide to commit crimes. Since my focus was on decision making, I have relied on rational choice theories in shaping the directions and questions for this study.

Economic Decision-Making Theory

Decision-making theory, first developed by mathematicians and economists, explains that individuals make decisions, whether of major or minor importance, based on information available to and known by them (Lee, 1971; Becker, 1976; Hill et al., 1979). No matter what the decision, whether it's going shopping today rather than tomorrow, traveling to Europe for the summer, or breaking into one house rather than another, decisions are made similarly by individuals who cognitively resolve "decision problems."

After defining and learning something about the problem, individuals theoretically identify and consider various alternative actions that realistically could be pursued. But, street criminals' alternatives are often few in number. They do not always have alternative courses of action of the quality or quantity available to law-abiding individuals with a "stake in conformity" (Hirschi, 1969). For example, their employment histories are typically erratic. Their relationships with family members are often strained, which leaves them without the support of a close primary group. Their opportunities for legitimately obtaining socially approved successes are not as numerous as for non-criminals.

After identifying and considering alternative actions, individuals theoretically compare the outcomes of one course of action to those of an alternative course of action. Both the calculations and outcomes are determined by individuals' short or long-term plans, their perceptions of the costs and rewards of the various behavior options, their personal preferences about particular courses of action, and their judgment as to whether the alternatives are viable and worthy of serious consideration. Decision makers implicitly assess the benefits that they hope to attain from a given course of action and compare those to benefits that may be derived from the alternatives. By assessing the benefits, individuals can then determine which of the alternative actions may generate the desired benefits and which may not. By failing to assess the various behavior options and the expected benefits from each, decisions may be less than optimal.

Optimal criminal and non-criminal decision making, according to the economic camp, results from rational calculations. For economists "accept as an article of faith, and assert as a revealed truth, the proposition that [humans are] rational, that [they are] free to choose among alternative behaviors, and that [their] choice[s are] governed by a desire to maximize [their] own well-being" (Orsagh, 1983: 392).

The economic conceptualization of rational *criminal* decision making is based on the idea that individuals are rational in their decisions to commit crimes, which implies that individuals have a realistic perception of both the probability of being sanctioned and of the severity of the sanction (i.e., risk) and that a criminal decision is a rational calculation of these factors rather than an impulsive, disorganized one. While the economic model has received criticism for its failure to predict individual choices, rational choice theorists usually attribute these failures to its inability to account for individuals' "cognitive limitations, short-cut decision making, and processing heuristics" (Lattimore and Witte, 1986: 133).

Cognitive Decision-Making Theory

Although economists posit rational decision making, cognitive psychology posits a less-than-rational approach by treating the decision maker as a "limited information processor" with various simplifying strategies for resolving decisions (Johnson and Payne, 1986: 180). When a limited information processor faces a decision, the decision is defined by "the acts or options among which one must choose, the possible outcomes or consequences of these acts, and the contingencies or conditional probabilities that relate outcomes to acts" (Tversky and Kahneman, 1981: 453). However, when individuals make choices about gains and losses, the imperfections of their perceptions often cloud the possible outcomes and contingencies of their decisions. Psychologists argue that since individuals act based on their subjective perceptions, they often do not act rationally or optimally (Goldberg, 1970; Gardner, 1985) and may fail to "make decisions that [are] objectively the best" (Clarke and Cornish, 1985: 159).

Psychologists believe that individuals' decisions are not as sophisticated as economists purport, and criticize economists for their inability to account for empirical decision making. Cognitive theorists claim that by suggesting that criminals are rational actors, economists imply that criminals have a realistic perception of the potential certainty and severity of punishment and act after rational calculation. Psychologists believe that they may act with limited rationality rather than full rationality (Cornish and Clarke, 1987), which implies that individuals' capacities to acquire and process information are limited. Individuals allegedly make a few simple and concrete examinations of their opportunities and make decisions that can be far short of optimal (Cook, 1980). Thus, decision makers, including those involved in criminal decision making, almost "invariably choose a course of action without knowing for certain what its consequences will be" (Hill et al., 1979). As a result, individuals do not necessarily "conceptualize the possible sanctions they face" and may not be easily deterred from committing crimes (Carroll, 1982: 57). The fact that people do not always make the most rational decisions, that they may pay undue attention to less important information, and that they employ shortcuts while processing information is relevant to an understanding of decision making, including criminal decision making (Clarke and Cornish, 1985: 160).

Perceptual Deterrence Theory

Criminologists historically have shown sustained interest in deterrence theory and research. Despite conceptual differences that pervade the diverse theoretical literature, a deterrence hypothesis has emerged: law violation is inversely related to the threat of legal punishment (Grasmick and Milligan, 1976). A fundamental premise of the deterrence hypothesis is that individual behavior is the product of rational deliberation about the expected risks and benefits of a particular course of action. According to deterrence theory, law-abiding individuals seek the benefits of conformity (e.g., network acceptance, social standing) and avoid the costs of deviance (e.g., network ostracism, self-embarrassment, legal penalties, loss of social standing). The expectation of social approval for conformity and punishment for deviance is an important variable in explaining conformity. Deterrence theory, however, emphasizes the fear of punishment and the law, shaped by external and internal controls, as the variable that best explains conformity to normative behavior (Hirschi, 1969). For deterrence theorists, then, formal punishment is designed not as retributive in nature but as social control, for it allegedly affects the future behavior of the punished individual specifically and society generally (Meier and Johnson, 1977; Gibbs, 1981).

In the past, criminologists largely ignored cognitive psychology and individual decision making (Clark and Cornish, 1985) but attention increasingly has focused on deviant behavior and the subjective methods used by individuals when deciding to commit crimes (e.g., Konecni et al., 1976; Carroll, 1978, 1982; Konecni and Ebbesen, 1979; Cook, 1980).

In recent years, deterrence theorists have emphasized the psychological processes of individuals' decision making, and perceptual deterrence, a rational-choice model of criminal decision making, has emerged. Perceptual deterrence theory, a hybrid of control, economic, and psychological decision-making theories, highlights the importance of the person's assessment of the potential costs and benefits of various behavior options.

Although this study was not a theory-testing study, these three related but divergent bodies of thought— economic, cognitive, and perceptual deterrence theories— served as theoretical guidance for this study of criminal decision making. In the following section, I briefly critique relevant empirical studies of criminal decision making.

A Critique of Decision-Making Research

Early deterrence and decision-making research focused on the relationship between aggregate crime rates and various operational definitions of the certainty and severity of punishment (e.g., Gibbs, 1968; Tittle, 1969; Jensen, 1969; Chiricos and Waldo, 1970; Bailey and Smith, 1972; Sjoquist, 1973; Bailey, 1975; Ehrlich, 1975; McPheters, 1976; Blumstein et al., 1978). Some studies found deterrent effects of certainty, but not severity of legal punishment[4] (Chambliss, 1966; Gibbs, 1968; Jensen, 1969; Tittle, 1969, 1980; Chiricos and Waldo, 1970; Waldo and Chiricos, 1972; Tittle and Rowe, 1977). Since early studies relied on aggregate data, they share a common fundamental weakness—they tell us little about the processes of individual criminal decision making and how risks of formal and informal punishment fit into an individual's criminal calculus. By contrast, perceptual deterrence research focuses specifically on individuals' assessments of the probability of sanction. However, previous perceptual deterrence research is limited due primarily to the methodologies of the studies. The study of individual criminal behavior has actually received little attention from both economic and cognitive decision-making researchers (e.g., Becker, 1968; Firey, 1969). When it has, the samples typically have had weaknesses similar to those in deterrence research—namely their weak generalizability to individuals engaged in actual decisions about crime. Three types of samples have been used in perceptual deterrence and decision-making studies—high school and college students (e.g., Waldo and Chiricos, 1972; Silberman, 1976; Erickson et al., 1977; Jensen et al., 1978; Jensen and Stitt, 1982; Paternoster et al., 1982a, 1982b, 1983; Rankin and Wells, 1983), adults who commit very minor crimes (e.g., traffic offenses, shoplifting, and income tax evasion) and whose actions are not met with grave informal or formal punishment (e.g., Grasmick and Milligan, 1976; Meier and Johnson, 1977; Grasmick and Bryjak, 1980; Brown, 1981; Buckle and Farrington, 1984; Grasmick, 1985; Green, 1985), and incarcerated offenders. The findings from samples of students, non-criminal adults, and incarcerated offenders cannot be generalized to individuals who repeatedly commit property or garden-variety crimes, or to the processes by which they decide to commit such crimes (Glassner and Carpenter, 1985).

Although studies using samples of incarcerated offenders inform us about the perceptions of individuals involved in serious crimes, they have focused on other issues and have used very limited data collection measures (e.g., Petersilia et al., 1978; Petersilia, 1980; Peterson et al., 1980). The majority of such studies relied on cross-sectional data produced from anonymous closed-ended questionnaires (e.g., Grasmick and Milligan, 1976; Erickson et al., 1977; Grasmick and Bryjak, 1980; Grasmick, 1985). Since these surveys relied on anonymity, data could not be compared to official criminal records, and hence validity and reliability of the findings have been subject to criticism (Jensen and Stitt, 1982). Surveys are further criticized for forcing participants to select a response option, and not allowing them to explain, in their own words, their criminal involvement, reasoning processes, thoughts about crime and punishment, and alternatives to the crime that they may have considered. Critics suggest using both data that are self-reported during in-depth interviews, and official measures of criminal behavior (Petersilia, 1980). Investigators, in the past, have neglected to examine respondents' explanations and elaborations of their perceptions and decision-making processes, and the issue of deterrence. However, interviews increasingly have been called for to measure deterrent effects and to assess individual decision making (e.g., Petersilia et al., 1978; Jensen et al., 1978; Jacob, 1979; Paternoster et al., 1982a; Richards and Tittle, 1982; Rankin and Wells, 1983; Shover, 1985; Glassner and Carpenter, 1985; Clark and Cornish, 1985; Piliavin et al., 1986; Tuck and Riley, 1986).

Since cross-sectional data relies on retrospective accounts, critics further contend that the temporal order of perceptions and behavior may be confused, and rather than measuring deterrent effects (i.e., where perceptions of outcomes affect behavior) previous studies may have actually measured experiential effects (i.e., where behavior affects perceptions of outcomes) (e.g., Grasmick and Bryjak, 1980; Jensen and Stitt 1982; Saltzman et al., 1982; Minor and Harry, 1982; Paternoster et al., 1983; Rankin and Wells, 1983; Paternoster et al., 1985; Piliavin et al., 1986; Paternoster, 1987). To overcome this methodological weakness, researchers recently have called for greater use of longitudinal studies to detect changes in individuals' perceptions of their circumstances and to allow for prospective predictions by the respondents (Farrington, 1979; Paternoster et al., 1983; 1985).

Still others inform us that cross-sectional measurements can be as reliable as longitudinal measurements if the researcher cautiously approaches the interview subjects, diligently attempts to establish a trusting relationship where rapport is meaningful, and is sensitive to causal ordering (Lundman, 1986). To accomplish this, the temporal sequence of events must be elaborated clearly. In this type of interview, a researcher would elicit information about the individual's retrospective thoughts and perceptions that occurred *prior* to a particular act, to establish such causal ordering.[5]

Studies of perceptual deterrence and individuals engaged in decision making have evaluated only target selection for various crimes (e.g., Maguire, 1980; Maguire and Bennett, 1982; Bennett and Wright, 1984a, 1984b; Akerstrom, 1985; Rengert and Wasilchick, 1985). In target selection research, individual criminals are called on to describe the appealing and unappealing properties of particular targets. Although these studies illustrate property offenders' methods of making decisions about whether to rob or burglarize a particular house or business, they, by design, ignore the individual's decision to commit or not commit the crime (e.g., Best and Luckenbill, 1982; Bennett and Wright, 1984a, 1984b). Doubtless, these decisions are interrelated, but they involve assessments of different decision problems. And the decision to commit or not commit a particular crime logically precedes both target selection and the actual crime.

In sum, studies of perceptual deterrence and individual decision making have increased our understanding of deterrence and decision making processes. However, the decision of choosing crime presently remains unexplored. Thus, my objective in this study was to gain a descriptive understanding of how individual repeat criminals make the decision to commit crimes, the various alternatives that they consider while deciding, and how the possibilities of both formal and informal punishment fit within their criminal calculus.

NOTES

1. I was among the lucky ones until, during the research for this book, my apartment was burglarized twice during a two-week period. Although never victimized before, I quickly came to understand how the victim feels and reacts to this kind of violation of space and privacy. But more important, I believe being twice victimized at the time that I was gave me a rare inside look at property crime—from both the offender's perspective, which I was learning during this study, and the victim's perspective, including, among others, the reactions of anger, fear, vulnerability, and resentment.

2. Although both the fear of crime and sales of crime-prevention commodities are increasing, recent research shows that property crime is not. During the 1980s, property crime remained relatively constant, with fewer households being victimized in 1989 than in previous years (Bureau of Justice, 1990a). For a more detailed explanation of this phenomenon, see Wright, 1985 and Tunnell, 1990a.

3. "Criminal calculus" is a rather vague term due to the way it has been used previously. The concept is derived from both the economic and cognitive approaches to understanding criminal behavior. It implies that individual criminals assess or calculate the potential costs and rewards of committing a particular crime. That is, individual criminals, theoretically, compare the benefits they believe they will gain from a crime against the risks they believe they may take when committing a crime. Likewise, they compare the perceived benefits from the crime under contemplation to the benefits they could obtain from other types of action, such as non-criminal behavior or another crime.

4. Of the three variables that allegedly produce a deterrent effect—certainty, severity, and celerity—certainty is without a doubt the most difficult for the state to manipulate. It is far easier for legislative bodies to simply increase the penalty severity for various crimes and to appropriate more funds for speedier judicial processing of criminal cases than to affect, in the least, the certainty of punishment, and even more difficult to affect the *perceptions* of increasing certainty of punishment.

5. A very recent study shows that longitudinal research has proven to offer more utility than cross-sectional research (Menard and Elliott, 1990). In fact, Menard and Elliott have this to say about the benefits of using a longitudinal research design:

> Longitudinal data allows us to generate strong tests of competing hypotheses which would be impossible without longitudinal data. We conclude that cross-sectional data, or longitudinal data collected in cross-sectional designs, are inadequate substitutions for prospectively collected data in the study of crime and delinquency (1990: 11).

My study, however, did not test theories or hypotheses and used a population that had actively engaged in crime in the past. Researchers may find that it is exceedingly difficult and perhaps impossible to obtain prospective data from active repeat offenders.

Methods and Procedures   2

Science is the description of experience.
—Ernst Mach, *The Science of Mechanics*

Numerous studies have been conducted within the research tradition of understanding risky decisions. As a result, I was able to make use of the cumulative knowledge about individuals' explanations of risk assessment. For example, we know something about risk perceptions for some deviant acts, but largely from the perspective of college and high school students. From earlier research, we have learned something about adults who commit minor criminal acts (e.g., traffic offenses and income tax evasion). But, these offenses do not represent acts of grave social concern; they are not considered socially harmful, and they are not actions that we as a society would like to contain. We have also learned something about the careers of habitual offenders; their explanations for their criminality, their entry into, persistence of, and desistance from their criminal careers. We also have learned something about historical and material conditions present when various criminal labels emerge and are applied to problem populations (e.g., Kramer, 1982). (See chapter 8, note 1 for a more detailed explanation.) From both this research tradition and the various case studies of individual criminals, we have gained some understanding of individual criminals, their criminal activity, and their explanations for committing crimes. My objective during this study, then, was not necessarily to examine issues addressed earlier but to build on previous studies and, as a result, move closer to understanding the process by which repeat offenders decide to commit crimes.

A central focus of this study was on the individual's criminal calculus. Although researchers have been less than clear on exactly what they mean by "criminal calculus" (see note 3 in chapter 1), for this research, criminal calculus refers to an individual criminal's assessment or calculation of his or her behavior options, including crime commission, and the perceived benefits from and consequences of committing a specific crime compared to those from another action (legitimate or illegitimate). Although we know various things about the risk-benefit calculus, we do not know how the criminal *decides* to commit a crime. That is what this research set out to determine.

The Sample

With the objective of exploring the decision-making process of the individual criminal, a sample of sixty property offenders was selected to shed new light on actual criminal decision making among chronic repeat offenders—the population responsible for committing a disproportionate number of property crimes. Each sample member was male, each was a repeat offender, and each was incarcerated in a Tennessee state prison.[1] Unlike samples used in previous research on making decisions about crime, this sample represents a population of ordinary repeat offenders who were once very active.

To ensure the selection of property criminals who had committed crimes repeatedly, four criteria were used. First, each sample member had to have been serving at least his second prison incarceration for felony property crimes.[2] By limiting the sample to those incarcerated two or more times, I am confident I increased the chances of including individuals who had committed a great number of crimes and with considerable frequency. I also believe that I decreased the chances of including first or second-time offenders (except the ones who

Table 2.1 Official Incarceration Histories[a]

Respondent[b]	Crime	Sentence	Date
1	Armed Robbery	5 yrs.	8/83
	Armed Robbery	10 yrs.	2/85
2	Dwelling Shooting	4–10 yrs.	3/76
	Forgery	1 yr.	5/83
	Burglary	7 yrs.	6/85
3	Armed Robbery	Life	2/74
	Forgery	3 yrs.	10/78
	Armed Robbery	10 yrs.	12/81
4	Burglary	3 yrs.	1/74
	Armed Robbery	25 yrs.	11/80
5	Auto Theft	2 yrs.	11/68
	Armed Robbery	25 yrs.	7/70
6	Mail Obstruction	90 days	5/78
	Burglary	3 yrs.	12/80
	Burglary	9 yrs.	8/81
7	Armed Robbery	10 yrs.	11/78
	Burglary	10 yrs.	6/85
8	Grand Theft	3 yrs.	8/78
	Grand Theft	3 yrs.	8/80
	Burglary	9 yrs.	7/84
9	Burglary	2 yrs.	7/65
	Attempted Robbery	1–3 yrs.	8/68
	Armed Robbery & Kidnapping	25 yrs.	12/78
10	Burglary	5–10 yrs.	5/76
	Burglary	10 yrs.	12/84
11	Petty Larceny	3–5 yrs.	3/49
	Assault	1–5 yrs.	12/53
	Robbery	10 yrs.	6/57
	Armed Robbery	20 yrs.	8/64
	Habitual Criminal	Life	8/64
12	Accessory to Murder	5 yrs.	5/80
	Burglary	9 yrs.	4/85
13	Burglary	5–7 yrs.	11/76
	Drug Possession	3 yrs.	8/85
	Robbery	5 yrs.	5/86

(continued on next page)

Table 2.1 *(continued)*

Respondent[b]	Crime	Sentence	Date
14	Burglary	3 yrs.	2/78
	Burglary	6 yrs.	2/86
15	Burglary	3 yrs.	12/73
	Armed Robbery	31 yrs.	7/77
	Burglary	12 yrs.	3/84
16	Robbery	5 yrs.	11/76
	Armed Robbery	20 yrs.	11/80
17	Robbery	3 yrs.	3/77
	Grand Theft	2 yrs.	3/84
	Robbery	6 yrs.	4/86
18	Concealing Stolen Property	3 yrs.	9/78
	Armed Robbery	10 yrs.	8/82
19	Forgery	5 yrs.	7/76
	Auto Theft	3–4 yrs.	11/81
	Burglary	7 yrs.	3/86
20	Larceny from a Bank	15 yrs.	10/70
	Armed Robbery	20 yrs.	9/82
21	Burglary	5 yrs.	11/80
	Burglary	4 yrs.	4/85
22	Passing Bad Checks	4.5 yrs.	4/81
	Forgery	1 yr.	9/83
	Burglary	10 yrs.	8/85
23	Larceny from a Person	3 yrs.	6/79
	Burglary	9 yrs.	3/83
24	Receiving Stolen Property	1–3 yrs.	5/65
	Burglary	3 yrs.	10/66
	Mail Theft	1.5 yrs.	7/71
	Burglary	5 yrs.	11/79
	Burglary	15 yrs.	2/83
25	Burglary	5 yrs.	3/80
	Burglary	10 yrs.	7/83
26	Auto Theft	1.5 yrs.	1/74
	Armed Robbery	5–8 yrs.	7/77
	Armed Robbery	15 yrs.	3/80
27	Attempted Burglary	2 yrs.	6/65
	Attempted Auto Theft	1.5–2.5 yrs.	5/68

Table 2.1 *(continued)*

Respondent[b]	Crime	Sentence	Date
	Burglary	3 yrs.	9/72
	Forgery	1–5 yrs.	10/74
	Burglary	17 yrs.	12/82
28	Forgery	2 yrs.	1/64
	Grand Larceny	2 yrs.	10/65
	Burglary	3 yrs.	11/68
	Concealing Stolen Property	3–10 yrs.	11/74
	Burglary	3 yrs.	2/82
	Receiving Stolen Property	5 yrs.	3/85
29	Burglary	6 yrs.	3/78
	Armed Robbery	15 yrs.	8/83
30	Petty Larceny	1 yr.	12/76
	Armed Robbery	7 yrs.	8/86
31	Grand Larceny	3–5 yrs.	10/61
	Petty Larceny	7 yrs.	7/65
	Bank Burglary	12 yrs.	4/68
	Petty Larceny	2 yrs.	11/74
	Concealing Stolen Property	2 yrs.	12/81
	Concealing Stolen Property	3 yrs.	11/82
	Burglary	13 yrs.	6/85
32	Receiving Stolen Property	1 yr.	4/73
	Armed Robbery	12 yrs.	12/83
33	Petty Theft	2 yrs.	3/77
	Armed Robbery	30 yrs.	8/81
34	Receiving Stolen Property	3 yrs.	6/75
	Burglary	10–15 yrs.	2/80
35	Forgery	3 yrs.	4/76
	Robbery	10 yrs.	8/85
36	Burglary	6–16 yrs.	1/81
	Burglary	7 yrs.	2/84
37	Auto Theft	3 yrs.	3/74
	Armed Robbery	30 yrs.	2/77
38	Burglary	5 yrs.	3/80
	Burglary	10 yrs.	2/83
39	Robbery	5 yrs.	10/68
	Armed Robbery	25 yrs.	12/74

(continued on next page)

Table 2.1 *(continued)*

Respondent[b]	Crime	Sentence	Date
40	Armed Robbery	10 yrs.	4/76
	Burglary	8 yrs.	8/85
41	Burglary	3 yrs.	7/79
	Burglary	7 yrs.	8/83
42	Grand Larceny	5 yrs.	9/82
	Burglary	4 yrs.	4/86
43	Burglary	3–5 yrs.	7/81
	Burglary	10 yrs.	9/83
44	Burglary	5 yrs.	6/80
	Burglary	8 yrs.	3/83
45	Auto Theft	5 yrs.	5/80
	Burglary	7 yrs.	9/83
46	Larceny	2 yrs.	7/81
	Burglary	10 yrs.	3/83
47	Forgery	6 mos.	3/71
	Counterfeiting	5 yrs.	6/75
	Burglary	10 yrs.	6/85
48	Selling Marijuana	1 yr.	3/78
	Armed Robbery	10 yrs.	4/80
	Burglary	15 yrs.	2/83
49	Auto Theft	3 yrs.	9/79
	Burglary	10 yrs.	6/83
50	Burglary	5 yrs.	5/81
	Burglary	10 yrs.	4/84
51	Burglary	5 yrs.	4/82
	Grand Larceny	3 yrs.	8/84
52	Burglary	3 yrs.	3/82
	Burglary	5 yrs.	6/84
53	Robbery	5 yrs.	2/65
	Mail Theft	2 yrs.	9/71
	Burglary	3 yrs.	7/79
	Armed Robbery	20 yrs.	7/81
54	Petty Larceny	2–5 yrs.	11/79
	Burglary	7 yrs.	8/83

Table 2.1 *(continued)*

Respondent[b]	Crime	Sentence	Date
55	Burglary	5 yrs.	2/80
	Burglary	5 yrs.	7/83
56	Burglary	3 yrs.	6/81
	Burglary	6 yrs.	11/83
57	Burglary	5 yrs.	4/77
	Burglary	4 yrs.	2/87
58	Robbery	3 yrs.	8/81
	Burglary	7 yrs.	4/83
59	Burglary	5 yrs.	2/81
	Receiving Stolen Property	5 yrs.	5/84
60	Burglary	5 yrs.	4/81
	Burglary	5 yrs.	3/84

a. These data were obtained from the participants' official state records and Federal Bureau of Investigation "rap sheets."

b. The respondents were randomly ordered and then assigned numbers in simple ascending order. The individuals who participated in this study cannot be identified by these numbers.

were either so unlucky or sloppy that they were caught, convicted, and imprisoned for every crime they committed). Table 2.1 shows the incarceration histories of the sixty sample members, including the sentences and dates they were sentenced. The official data in this table tell us about the types of crimes they committed and the frequency with which they came under official detection.

The second criterion for sample selection was that one of their two incarcerations had to have been for either burglary or armed robbery.[3] Since burglary and armed robbery account for the majority of serious property crimes reported yearly, they represent those criminal acts that we as a society are consistently concerned about (Uniform Crime Reports, 1986; Flanagan and Jamieson, 1988). Thus, to ensure inclusion of serious property offenders in the sample, those selected had to have been incarcerated for one of the two most commonly occurring serious property crimes.

The third criterion for selecting a sample was that the participants had to have been at least twenty-five years of age. The rationale for this criterion was that sample members could not have committed crimes over an extended period of time and with any frequency at less than twenty-five years of age. This minimum age criterion was also set to increase the likelihood of obtaining information from the participants that was dependent on self-reflection. Such self-reflection often comes with maturity and age and, as a result, typically eludes young adults. By setting a minimum age of twenty-five, I increased the odds of getting rich, detailed descriptions of their reasoning for choosing crime.

The fourth criterion was to limit the sample to males, since research shows that males account for the great majority of all serious property crimes and that females traditionally have not been actively involved in burglaries and armed robberies (Mann, 1984; Morris, 1987). Thus, males offered a good opportunity to understand the decision-making processes of repetitive property criminals.[4] Table 2.2 illustrates the demographics for this sample.

Data Collection

I used three methods of data collection in this study—official state records, loosely structured personal interviews, and field notes. These three methods were used to understand the subtleties and dynamics of offenders' decision-making processes in a way that quantitative or aggregate data would not allow, and added an internal validity check (Burgess, 1982).

The first data collection was done before I met with the participants. I reviewed their official arrest and incarceration records to determine if each met the sample criteria and to have an "official" record of their arrest and incarceration histories (see table 2.1). When the participants told me about their arrests and incarcerations, I resolved any contradictions that arose between the official record and their self-reporting. My objective in collecting official data was to have an accurate history of their contacts with the criminal justice system, including the frequency and results of those contacts.

Methods and Procedures 21

Table 2.2   Sample Demographics

	Mean
Age	34
Years of education	10
Age at first arrest	11

Race composition: 38 white and 22 black participants
N = 60

The Board of Parole allowed me access to their files and some information on data base. As I reviewed the list of those about to be released, I looked for inmates who were incarcerated for property crimes and requested their files from the state records office. I then scrutinized the files to determine if the inmates met the sample criteria. If they did, I assembled a fairly detailed history of their criminal activity, including their arrests and incarcerations.[5]

The second method of collecting data, and certainly the most fruitful for the objectives of this study, was the personal interview, which I conducted with the participants to elicit detailed accounts of the processes by which they decided to commit specific crimes (McCracken, 1988). I used an interview guide to ensure that each participant was asked similar information and audiotaped each interview. In an effort to understand the criminal calculus, I had each participant describe the way he cognitively framed and resolved a typical, specific decision to commit a crime. Each was questioned about and described the way he gathered and defined information about whether to commit a crime; the various alternatives considered to the crime; his knowledge of such alternatives; the process by which alternatives were evaluated; and perceptions of the costs and rewards of one alternative over another. By focusing on these specific processes, I attempted to situate their criminal decision making within a theoretical context guided by deterrence and rational-choice theories.

As I interviewed the participants, I tried to make them feel as though they possessed knowledge unknown to those outside their profession (Hammersley and Atkinson, 1983). To accomplish this, I followed the lead of an earlier researcher who interviewed inmates on Alabama's death row and had this to say about the interviewer-interviewee relationship:

> By placing individuals in a role that approximates that of a co-researcher into their personal difficulties, they are provided with a motivation for introspection (Johnson, 1981:13).

Thus, I strove to shape and focus the interviews through conversations, sometimes painful, sometimes humorous, but nonetheless, focused, in which I acted as a conversational guide. I became an active listener, and constantly assessed how what I heard related to the focus of the research and how it was similar or dissimilar to what other respondents had told me. By using a respectful yet critical approach, I also monitored reliability by letting the participants know that I was "conwise" if certain information appeared dubious or contrary to official documentation (Frazier, 1978).

My objective was to "'get inside the head'" of each participant, which could only be accomplished through long interviews that produced richly detailed information—interviews that demanded the approach and sensitivity that Lofland and Lofland suggest.

> Intensive interviewing . . . is a guided conversation . . . to elicit from the interviewee rich, detailed materials . . . to discover the informant's experience of a particular topic or situation (1984: 12-13).

The third method of data collection was the analytical memos or field notes that were written or dictated after nearly every interview and at any other occasion when inspiration came over me or as I struggled with an emerging pattern. The notes were used to make analytic "sense" of the information as it came in and especially as it related to the criminal calculus (e.g., Glaser, 1978; Lofland and Lofland, 1984; Sanjek, 1990). The field notes were not only used to assess progress in analyzing the phenomenological information, but also allowed for emergent ideas to be identified and research strategies and lines of inquiry to be developed and pursued with the participants (Johnson and Johnson, 1990). I am convinced that without the use of these notes and the constant analytical thinking about the data that such note-keeping mandates, the data would have been lost and little would have been learned from the research.

The Interview Setting

During the several months of conducting interviews, I visited six state prisons, three minimum-security community service institutions, two work camps, and five county jails in the state of Tennessee. Although no two prisons are alike, they do share several commonalities. For example, all appear very cold, brutal, and dark—the end of the line, desolate, lonely places to live. The majority of the prisons I visited are situated in rural, out-of-the-way places, the kinds of places that caused me to put myself in the shoes of the prisoners and wonder what it must feel like to be sentenced to several years of confinement there, away from civilization as the prisoners know it. Since so many prisoners are from urban settings, the process of driving through open country to their place of confinement must feel as though they are leaving this world and being taken to an alien environment—one that is foreign to them and that they have very little control over.

The main prison in Nashville was built in the mid 1800s and its architecture reflects the prison design of that era. It is a gray, gothic, castle-like, concrete and brick structure with enormous turrets. Had it been anything other than a prison, I am confident it would have displayed gargoyles. The windows in the front of the prison (an area reserved for trustees) are very large, larger than windows found in elementary schools from the early part of this century, and covered with bars. In the bowels of the prison there are no windows.

Tennessee's most famous prison, Brushy Mountain, is just outside Petros in the heart of coal country in east Tennessee.[6] The road from Petros winds uphill toward the mountains and literally ends at the front of the prison. The prison's natural setting reminds one of a boxed canyon, with the front entrance to the prison built at the opening of the canyon and the living and yard areas built inside the canyon itself. Nothing but mountainous, tree-covered terrain surrounds the prisoners' home for the next several years. This institution has served as Tennessee's maximum-security prison for the majority of its existence. For a period of time, it served as a general population prison, including when I visited there in December 1986 and a few times in 1987. As Brushy Mountain made its conversion from a maximum-security to a general population prison, it did not necessarily relax its security strategies, although in all of my five or six visits, I was never searched before being given entry.[7] Brushy still looks ominously threatening, and life there is more rugged than at most other prisons. The prison, located in the Cumberland Mountains, experiences cold winters and damp, cold fogs that last until late morning. Brushy's reputation is built on its natural setting, which prevents successful escapes, but nearly all the Tennessee prisons function similarly, if by nothing more than their isolated and rural settings.

The regional prisons that I visited are little more than work camps, prisons with enormous acreage where inmates are expected to work in one of a number of jobs, from industrial to farm-related. A significant number of inmates do little more than cut weeds with hand-held scythes. They related to me how useless they believed their work was and how they could learn other skills, if only the state would adopt certain educational and training policies. These inmates, like those at Brushy Mountain, typically were far from their homes and families, who have difficulty visiting easily or regularly.

A few of the inmates were being held in county jails at the time of the interviews.[8] I visited jails in five different counties. Although prisons are horrible places to live and visit, jails are worse. They are constantly noisy, they smell, the quarters are close and confining, and inmates have little privacy. There is no work there, nothing to occupy their time, and nothing that affords them the chance to feel as though they are contributing to anything. The inmates tend to feel like pariahs. Jails were also those places where the inmate and I had the least privacy and where the interview audiotape consistently recorded not only our conversations but also a host of background goings on—men yelling, radios playing, steel doors slamming, bells ringing, and guards talking. These sounds are part of the normal atmosphere of jails.

The most relaxed and least offensive prisons were those classified as community corrections centers. I visited three of the four in the state and found them certainly minimum-security institutions. Many inmates worked full-time away from the institution and returned to the prison only in the evenings. They had a different air about them than inmates confined to more restrictive institutions. Prisoners there related to me how they enjoyed considerable autonomy and how things in their lives were improving. The front-line prison guards also seemed fairly relaxed there, especially compared to county jails.

I always arranged in advance with an assistant warden or a prison coordinator to visit a particular inmate at a specific date and time. After my arrival at the prison, I made my way to the first check point.[9] It was at the inside check point that the decision was made whether to search me or not. During those times when the decision was made to search me, I was asked to empty my pockets and put my research materials on the countertop. Searching my possessions varied considerably from guard to guard. Some would merely glance at the items, some would quickly leaf through my papers, and some searched with such confidence in their suspicions that I had to be carrying contraband that they actually disassembled (as best they could) my tape recorder, audio cassette tape boxes, leafed through the various papers that I had for the interview and my wallet, and on two occasions counted my money.

The prison staff usually did an adequate job of communicating with each other, for the front-line personnel nearly always had the information from the assistant warden that I would arrive on that date, at that time, to interview a particular inmate. On those rare occasions when they had not received a memo, a phone call was all that it took to clear up the lack of communication. At least twice, however, the inmate had not been told of my arriving on a specific day and was somewhere away from prison working for the day. There was nothing I could do during those times; they represented wasted trips and lost hours driving to and fro. I tried to arrive at the prison at a time that allowed the interview to take place without interruption; for example, I avoided lunch time.[10] If all went well, I would be escorted to a small room usually used for other forms of consultation, where I waited for the prisoner to be escorted to our meeting.

Shortly thereafter, a guard would enter escorting a prisoner.[11] Although a heterogeneous group, similar first impressions of these men were inevitable. They shared the appearance of being downtrodden, lethargic, easily movable from place to place (much like cattle herded wherever they go), fairly soft-spoken, suspicious, passive conversationalists, tattooed, often dirty, and hollow-eyed.

I always began by thanking the guard for his/her help and then would turn to the prisoner and introduce myself, shake his hand, and ask if he had received the letter about the project.[12] Then I would remind him of what he had read in the letter and explain in much greater detail the research project, his selection as a potential participant, the types of information that I was seeking, the process of tape-recording the interview, the amount of time required for the interview, his rights as a participant, issues of confidentiality, and monetary compensation for participating. I would then communicate that I would be happy to answer any questions the prisoner might have.[13] Those who agreed to participate signed an informed consent form, keeping a copy for themselves.[14] The interview, which lasted from one to three hours, would then begin and usually take place within a small counseling room.[15] It was during this interview that I had each participant describe the process by which he decided to commit a crime.

Data Analysis

The interviews with each participant were audiotaped and later transcribed. While reading the transcripts, I searched for information pertinent to the research objectives and for patterns among the participants. Those dialogues were then subjected to qualitative data analyses to better understand criminal decision making, to understand its changing character, and to develop taxonomies of offender decision making.

Data were gathered and kept in the form of field notes. From the notes and interviews, I constructed types of decision making that were often revised with a variety of characters and names. I finally opted for using the labels *persistent* and *sporadic* decision makers. Briefly (for these are explicated in chapter 8), the *persistent* is a very active high-rate offender, that is, one who has not only committed a great number of felonies (at least one hundred during his lifetime), but also at a fairly intensive frequency. The *sporadic* is less active and less committed to a criminal lifestyle. He has committed less than one hundred felonies across his lifetime and at a less frequent rate than the persistent. These criminal decision-making types represent both quantitative and qualitative differences in criminal activity and decision making.

The final data analysis technique involved simple reconstructions of each offender's criminal history, including his arrests and incarcerations, which I had done prior to the interview. This analysis was a descriptive one where a complete history was assembled for each of the sixty respondents. These reconstructions included compilations of incarceration histories (see table 2.1) and sample demographics (see table 2.2). With the foreknowledge of the known crimes each respondent had committed and the frequency with which he had come into contact with the criminal justice system, I asked each offender for the total number and types of crimes he had committed, both those for which he had been arrested and those that had escaped official detection. The types and number of self-reported crimes committed by this sample are found in table 2.3. Judging from their reports, this sample was very active criminally. Although these numbers are shockingly high, other research has reported criminals committing as many as fifty-three armed robberies and ninety burglaries yearly, similarly high figures (Greenwood, 1982).

Although these methods represent mainstream social science methods, their use with this particular population is unique. We as a society want and need to understand the behavior of this population to aid in forming public policy that is both just and well-informed. This research and these methods bring us as close as we have come to understanding the actual

Table 2.3 Total Number of Self-Reported Crimes[a]

Crime Type	Number of Offenders	Total Number Committed
Armed Robbery	29	1,080
Strong-Armed Robbery	17	907
Residential Burglary	43[b]	5,011
Business Burglary	43[c]	2,441
Auto Theft	37	3,400
Shoplifting	40	4,040
Buying and Selling Stolen Goods	43	13,946
Forgery	24	6,441
Grand Theft	41	7,581
Petty Theft	38	3,879
Total number of crimes committed		48,726

a. These data represent self-report data. The participants were asked if they had committed each of these crimes. If the answer was affirmative, they were then asked how many they had committed as a juvenile, as a young adult, and as an adult. (Juvenile period refers to younger than age 18; young adult period refers to the ages 18–26; adult period refers to age 27 and older.) The only possible validity check was to compare the types of crimes they reported committing to their official arrest and incarceration records. If they reported committing several burglaries, I expected to find some indication of activity in burglary among their official arrest records.
b. 9 of the 43 reported they committed no business burglaries
c. 8 of the 43 reported they committed no residential burglaries

decision of chronic repetitive criminals to commit a crime. The only method that would bring us any closer would be for the researcher to act as a participant observer in both criminal decision making and actual crime commission. Yet questions of ethics, access to the actual crime, and investigator responsibility may prevent this inside look for some time.

A Look Ahead

The following chapters offer qualitative data on several specific issues related to criminals' decision making. Chapter 3 describes the respondents' accounts of their motivations for committing ordinary property crimes. Chapter 4 describes the alternatives that they not only defined as available to them but considered as they made decisions to commit crimes. Chapter 5 describes their use of neutralization techniques that aided them in their decisions to engage in specific crimes. Chapter 6 describes, from the interview data, the actual decision to commit a crime. These descriptions explicate the participants' thoughts of official and unofficial sanctions and the benefits they expected to obtain from crime; that is, it explains their criminal calculus. Chapter 7 describes, from the interview data, the thinking that went on when they decided *not* to commit a crime.

After these general findings are discussed in the next few chapters, they are related to specific decision-making types constructed from this sample. These decision-making types, along with a case study of each are found in chapter 8. Chapter 9 relates the data findings and analyses to current public policy and offers new directions for a just, humane, and well-informed public policy.

NOTES

1. Due to overcrowded conditions in Tennessee prisons, some state prisoners incarcerated for felony convictions are held in local jails. In fact, recent research shows that 25 percent of all state inmates in Tennessee are held in local jails due to overcrowding (Bureau of Justice, 1990b). As a result, a few of the participants who were interviewed were incarcerated as state prisoners in county jails.

Since each sample member was male, the pronouns "he" and "his" will be used in the remainder of this work when referring specifically to this sample.

2. Since this is a purposive, non-probability sample, representativeness can only be assumed, not determined. This study, like all studies using only one population from one setting at one time, can be criticized for lacking external validity. Thus, application of this study's results to a broader sample of property criminals is not justifiable methodologically.

Because of the complications of sampling among a population of criminals and the limitations thereof, two provisos are necessary. First, the sample members were "ordinary" because they had committed those ordinary crimes that typically result in substantial prison sentences upon conviction. Generalizations to other types of criminals (e.g., white collar) would be unjustified. Second, the sample members were at least two-time losers, meaning they had been arrested and incarcerated twice. Generalizations to a more successful population (e.g., "professional" criminals) also would be unjustified.

Social scientists' options for selecting a more representative sample of repetitive criminals are few in number. We could attempt innovative methods for sample selections. For example, we could make connections, but not easily, with active criminals who we are confident commit crimes repeatedly. Or we could advertise, but with little hope of generating interest, in the classified sections of daily newspapers for repetitive property criminals. However we choose to select samples for understanding this problem population, we can be only so confident in our notions of representativeness (e.g., Becker, 1986).

3. There is much debate over classifying armed robbery as a property crime. The FBI indexes armed robbery as a violent crime against a person and not against property. But, the motivations and objectives of armed robbers are to gain property from their crimes and not necessarily to inflict physical injury. The FBI's own definition of robbery states *first* that it is an act of theft:

> "Robbery is the taking or attempting to take anything of value from the care, custody, or control of a person or persons by force or threat of force or violence and/or by putting the victim in fear" (Uniform Crime Reports, 1988: 18).

Although the use of force is a component of armed robbery, theft is the offender's objective and the victims of armed robberies are rarely injured during such crimes. In fact, recent Justice Department statistics show that individuals are injured in only 1.5 percent of all completed armed robberies (Jamieson and Flanagan, 1989).

4. A fifth criterion was also used but is rather unimportant to my research and this book. The research for this book was part of a larger project funded by the National Institute of Justice (Grant #86-NIJ-CX0068). The project's objectives were two-fold—to learn about decision making among repetitive property criminals, and to examine the relationship between aging and desistance from crime. The other investigators in the project explored the "age-desistance" question. My research interest was in the decision-making area. The fifth criterion, used only to generate a sample by which the age-desistance question could be explored, was that each sample member must have been approved for parole and have a release date not to exceed four months after the interview in prison. They were interviewed twice—once in

Methods and Procedures 31

prison and once nine months after their release. Research in criminal recidivism shows that most recidivists are reincarcerated within six to nine months after their release (Beck and Shipley, 1987). Therefore, recidivists among the sample members would more than likely have had opportunity to commit crimes prior to the second interview. The second interview, which examined their criminal activity since their release from prison, focused on those types of crimes they had considered committing and those types of crimes they had committed. Interestingly enough, fourteen of the sixty were reincarcerated within nine months of their release although seven of the fourteen were reincarcerated on new criminal charges and seven were reincarcerated for technical parole violations (e.g., curfew violations, leaving town for a weekend without permission). Of the other forty-six, two refused to participate in the follow-up interview, one had died, and one had escaped shortly after the first interview and had not been heard from since. A total of forty-six of the original sixty were interviewed a second time. Other than the seven who had been reincarcerated on new criminal charges, none admitted to committing any crimes since their release from prison. I am convinced that they had not all "gone straight" but preferred to not reveal anything to anyone in a position of perceived authority about their illegal activities since their release from prison.

Given the five criteria, filling the target sample of sixty was no easy task. Unlike assumptions made from news reports of the revolving door in the criminal justice system, property criminals serving their second prison sentences are not being discharged frequently and "getting off." These sixty were discovered only after sixteen trips to the Board of Parole in Nashville and after perusal of 357 potential sample members' case files. As the names of those meeting the sample criteria trickled in, they were contacted and visited at their place of incarceration. Although only fifteen individuals refused to participate, it surprisingly took eighteen months to fill the target sample of sixty.

5. This was no easy task because the case files were often disorganized, falling apart, incomplete, or simply missing-in-action. I was only somewhat surprised at the condition of the state files because I had had firsthand experience with state government and its record-keeping. A few years before researching this topic, I had worked for a state agency, one that required the same volume of paper work and record-keeping as the Department of Corrections and Board of Parole. I was accustomed to the disarray of case files that results from agencies that consistently employ too few people to competently do

the job and where pay is low and morale lower. The blame for poor records management is not on front-line workers, but rather on the policies of a state government and its agencies that continuously allow enormous employee turnover, too much work, too little pay, low morale problems, and next to no input from workers about the nature of their work.

6. Brushy Mountain prison is Tennessee's most famous for at least three reasons. First, due to its sheer isolated and rural setting, most inmates historically have considered it a very undesirable and brutal place to do time. Second, it traditionally has served as Tennessee's maximum-security prison, where individuals representing security threats were placed and often forgotten. Today, although no longer the maximum-security prison that it once was, there are holdovers from the way the prison was earlier run. For example, only at Brushy did several inmates report to me that prison guards still carry big sticks and use them on those inmates defined as "discipline problems." Third, Brushy Mountain has housed Tennessee's most famous prisoner—James Earl Ray—during the majority of his incarceration. He has spent a great deal of his imprisonment in self-imposed solitary confinement, surfacing only rarely (once to testify in Washington about the alleged conspiracy to kill Dr. Martin Luther King, Jr. and again when he was hospitalized after being stabbed repeatedly by several inmates in the prison library).

7. The process of searching every individual who goes beyond the central command post (in the front of the prison) has been used by prisons for decades now. Searches are made of correctional officers, prison counselors, ministers, lawyers, family members, and any "free world" person desiring entry. Oddly enough, I typically was searched more thoroughly at county jails than at maximum-security institutions. The community service institutions were also relaxed about the security of both the inmates and the "free world" people coming into the prisons. Thus, I rarely was searched at the minimum-security prisons. The main prison and the Reception and Classification Center in Nashville, Turney Center, and the work camps closely adhered to searching procedures. It was at those prisons that I was made to feel the most suspect not only by the searching but by the general attitude toward me as both a "free world" person and as a social science researcher. One reason for this rigid enforcement of prison search policies at these places may have been that my identity as social science researcher was redefined by front-line prison personnel as "liberal," "do-gooder," "pointy-head" or some other epithet

of disgust, suspicion or one representing the complete lack of faith that a great number of prison workers have in social science, social work, social services, or nearly anything else involving the word "social."

It was obvious on more than one occasion that prison guards had absolutely no confidence in research on the criminal's perspective. I had discovered that whenever a guard questioned me about this research, he or she nearly always assumed that the research results might have some effect on crime reduction or might be used in rehabilitation. One guard in particular asked me what I was researching. I gave him a cursory answer, enough, I thought, to satisfy him, for I knew he didn't really want a fairly exhaustive answer. After my quick reply, he said, "I know how we can deal with these thugs," at which point he raised his right hand into the air, put his hand into the shape of a handgun, and said, "Pow."

8. Inmates in Tennessee, as in other states, are scattered throughout the state in any place where there is room. Tennessee prisoners won a class-action suit against the state for imprisoning them in overcrowded conditions (*Scotty Grubbs et al. v. Jeff Reynolds and the Tennessee Department of Corrections*, 1983). Since that time, state prisoners increasingly have been housed in county jails.

9. I always drove a university car on these trips. The presence of an official state car with an official state logo on both front doors added legitimacy to my mission in the eyes of the front-line prison employees. Had I arrived in my own personal vehicle, this legitimacy would have been nonexistent and I would have been considered more suspect than I was anyway. The university car also allowed me to park near the front door in the "Official Visitor" parking space. I was nearly always seen as I parked my car (sometimes before if the watch towers were staffed). This obvious presence alerted the guards that I indeed was on official business, which I believe resulted in my being harassed less than I would have been had I arrived in no apparent official capacity.

10. Meals, I quickly discovered, are considered one of the bright spots of the day for most inmates. A few times, we had to break off the interview for the inmate to eat lunch and then continue after he had finished. Also, some inmates wanted to eat before the interview began, a request that meant waiting until the cafeteria opened and they had eaten.

11. On two occasions, both in the same county jail, the prisoner was brought into the room wearing both handcuffs and ankle shack-

les. I immediately asked the guard to remove the restraints. Both times the guard removed the handcuffs but refused to remove the shackles. Other than these two times, no prisoner was restrained in any way. There was never a time when I felt the least bit frightened by these prisoners or apprehensive about talking with them.

12. I always asked about the letter up front for two reasons. First, to connect my presence with the letter informing them that I would visit them soon. Second, to alleviate any worries or fears they might have that I was "the man," a member of the parole board, an attorney, or any other person in a position of control over them and their destiny. When I inquired about the letter, only one had not received it. He, nonetheless, agreed to participate.

It was also at this point that I would ask or encourage the guard to leave us in privacy. Only once, at a particularly inhospitable prison, did a guard stay in the room and listen to this introduction and to the informed consent procedure.

13. Each respondent was paid fifty dollars after the prison interview. Since prison rules prohibit checks being mailed to prisoners, and prisoners possessing more than a fixed amount of money, each respondent and I had to arrange to have his check mailed to a trusted relative or friend in the "free world" who could then cash the check and deliver the money in small increments to them or deposit it in a bank account for them. The participants were paid one-hundred dollars after the second interview (i.e., the interview that took place nine months after their release from prison). The increase in payment was to function as an incentive for them to keep in touch with us and to let us know of any address changes. Payment was made by check through the university. These payments were subsidized by research monies from the National Institute of Justice.

The most often asked question was if I could pay them in cash then and there. After I explained to them that I could not for two reasons (direct payment to Tennessee prisoners is forbidden and the money was handled by the university) they typically would roll their eyes and communicate that they understood the logic of bureaucracies. They felt reassured after learning that the payment would be made within two weeks.

14. At a couple of prisons, guards asked me to have the inmates sign the prison's version of an informed consent form. Their version, however, said that the state had access to the data and that anything the inmate said could be held against him in a court of law. I refused to comply with their request and on both occasions we had to discuss the matter with staff members who had more authority. Both times

Methods and Procedures

the prison staff relented and asked for a copy of our version of the informed consent form. I was happy to supply them with one.

15. I say "usually" because prisons do not have ample interviewing space other than that for prison personnel. I also interviewed in such diverse settings as a holding cell, a glass-enclosed room, a prison library, a warden's office, a parole board hearing room, a large broom closet, a prison chapel, a prison counselor's office, and an outdoor picnic area. Regardless, I was and am confident that we had complete privacy and that the participants also believed we did.

3 The Motivation To Commit Property Crime

> You wanna know why, I did what I did,
> I guess there's just a meanness, in this world.
> —Bruce Springsteen, "Nebraska"

Rational choice theorists assume that individual decision makers analytically resolve decision problems through a logically calculated series of steps that culminate in a rational decision. As a way of situating this research within a larger theoretical tradition, this study relied on social-psychological variables indicative of these steps that lead to rational decisions. The process of deciding and the various steps involved constitute the focus of this study and the components of such processes served as lines of inquiry.

During the in-depth interviews, I had each of the sixty participants reconstruct specific criminal decision problems and their resolutions. To this end, each participant was asked to recall the most recent typical crime he had committed and could remember clearly.[1] Once they had selected the most recent crime, all of the daily events, conversations, and thoughts which occurred during the decision to commit the crime were reconstructed through conversation. The conversations produced sixty crime-specific decision problems, and the way they were framed and resolved.

One of the earliest factors in the temporal process of deciding to commit a crime is the dimension of motivation. During the interviews, I occasionally posed the question simply as, "Why did you break into that house that day?" Sometimes I arrived at the information in less direct ways, by deducing motivation from the various topics of conversation about the day of the crime and its events.

As I describe the motivations to commit crime among this sample of repetitive property criminals in this chapter, decision-making theorists might be rather disappointed that the accounts offered by these prisoners are neither complex nor analytically sophisticated. But, these criminals may not be the most reflective individuals, who rational choice theorists may desire studying. They may have given little thought to motivational forces in their lives, and in this way are not unlike "normal," law-abiding individuals, who, might also be hard-pressed to explain the reasons for their actions and the choices they have made. Nonetheless, with this type of self-reporting retrospective research, we are left with little choice but to rely on the respondents for enlightening us as to motivation.

Motivations: Framing the Decision Problem

Social psychologists inform us that motivation is inseparable from goal attainment. Motivation research focuses primarily on the various factors that determine what psychologists call "goal-directed behavior," which is of central importance in understanding motivated behavior. "Motivated behavior can perhaps best be described by its purposefulness and persistence until the goal is reached" (Van Doren, 1972: 369) and such behavior usually will continue if the results are beneficial or positive. An attempt at goal attainment generally is preceded by the expectation of an end product—the perception of expected benefits from a particular act—and is the motivation for engaging in such an act. However, to analytically understand individuals' motivations is difficult, for motivation cannot be observed directly and must be inferred from either observed behavior or individuals' self-reporting of prebehavioral thoughts and perceptions of goals.

Motive is considered an essential component of criminal-

Table 3.1 Motivations to Commit Crime

Motivation Type	Number	Percent
Money	53	88
A sense of accomplishment	3	5
Crime as sport	2	3
Vengeance	2	3
Crime as power	3	5

The total number is greater than the N of 60 and the total percent is greater than 100 due to some overlap among the sample members' reporting.

ity by both jurists and investigators of criminal decision making. Jurists are interested in motivation because to them it represents an integral part of intent or *mens rea*. Decision-making researchers are interested in motivation because it represents a component of the decision problem: the benefits and calculable results the decision maker anticipates from engaging in a particular act.

It's Money that Matters

The motivating force among this sample of repetitive property criminals was nearly uniform—money—"quick, easy money," which they believed they would obtain from committing crimes. Table 3.1 illustrates the motivations to commit crime among this sample.

In fact, fifty three of the sixty (88 percent) reported that money was their primary motivating force for committing property crimes, as the following conversation with a twenty seven-year-old high-rate burglar illustrates.[2]

Q: Why do you think you did the armed robbery?
A: For the money.
Q: Any other reason?
A: I just wanted money.

The financial payoff from crime was defined as especially attractive when compared to the wages they would have expected, perhaps from past experience, to legally earn. The following brief excerpts from conversations with three of the sixty participants are illustrative of this primary motivation. I asked the following of a thirty-one-year-old high-rate burglar who was quite aware of the possibility of his earning a decent legitimate wage:

> Q: What about crime is attractive to you or appealing?
> A: It doesn't take very long, the profit is quick. If I worked construction I would make a week what I could make in fifteen minutes. That's pretty much why it's appealing.

The following dialogue with a twenty-nine-year-old burglar illustrates how money acted as the only benefit that he and others like him believed they would obtain from committing crimes.

> Q: So, when you were doing these burglaries then, what benefits did you see coming from them?
> A: The money to make it from day to day, to pay me gas, pot, party money. To have a good time.
> Q: Some people say they break into places for the thrill of it or the excitement or the accomplishment of it.
> A: It never gave me no thrill and I really wasn't accomplishing nothing but putting money in my pocket. So, I didn't get no thrill because of it.

The attractive benefits of criminality are illustrated in the following conversation with a high-rate burglar.

> Q: So it sounds like you're saying that the money you've made illegally far outweighs the money you can make—
> A: Far outweighs. I don't mind working, but it's hard to work all day and kill yourself for really nothing.

And the following conversation with a thirty-eight-year-old armed robber who began his criminal activities with shoplifting also illustrates the benefits of earning money through crime.

The Motivation to Commit Property Crime

Q: What benefit did you see coming from shoplifting and committing other crimes?
A: Just getting money to run around on the weekends with and buy some beer and whiskey and shit like that.

The financial attractiveness, coupled with the perception that threats of formal sanction were not serious, explains a significant part of the decision-making processes found among many of these respondents, particularly the high-rate persistent offenders.

Benefits identified other than money included the excitement of committing crime, the enjoyment of "getting over on" the powers that be, respect from peers for committing crime, and the control over crime situations and crime victims.[3] These anticipated benefits, however, represent *latent* benefits and not the prime objective considered as these men resolved criminal decision problems. The following dialogue with a twenty-eight-year-old high school dropout who had committed dozens of burglaries and auto thefts illustrates this point.

Q: What was the reason you did the burglary?
A: Well, for the money, for the money. That's the only reason I did any burglaries. Really, any crime at all would be for the money. And the excitement, you know, it was always there, but it was for the money, more or less.
Q: Did you see any other benefits coming from doing burglaries or was it just the money?
A: Just the money.
Q: You didn't do it because it was exciting or—
A: It was fun, I guess it was kind of exciting in a way.

We can see from the above dialogue that money represented the primary motivation and expected benefit from this crime. Excitement was present but only as a latent benefit—a byproduct of the criminal act.

Although excitement did contribute to the motivation for some of these offenders, the burglar in the following dialogue claimed that for him excitement was not an issue.

Q: Why did you do it, for the money, or excitement, or—
A: Oh, for the money and no, I don't think it was for the excitement, it was just for the money.

Although some of these criminals had very few living expenses (they lived either at home with their parents, with a spouse or lover who worked, or with a series of lovers), they wanted "easy money" to spend on leisure and recreational activities. This twenty-nine-year-old burglar, who rarely worked a legitimate job, reported this when I questioned him about motivation:

Q: Why did you do the burglary?
A: Broke and needed money and wasn't working. And just needed money to drink and party. It wasn't for bills.

As previous research has likewise shown (e.g., Petersilia et al., 1978), money represents the most common motivation. In fact, fifty-three reported that money was nearly the only element that motivated them to commit crimes. However, nearly a third of the sample (N = seventeen or 32 percent) sought money because they had severe physical drug addictions. Their motive was to obtain money to purchase a drug to which they were literally physically addicted (or they defined their situation as such) and they committed crimes to sustain an addiction to a very expensive drug, not necessarily as a "way of life." The following conversation with a thirty-three-year-old individual who committed a wide variety of crimes, but tended to specialize in a particular crime type for a period of time, sheds light on the motivating power of money for drugs.

Q: Why did you commit forgeries at that time?
A: The reason was to get money to buy the drugs with.
Q: That was the main reason?
A: That was the only reason.
Q: Did you use a lot of drugs?
A: Constantly. It was money for drugs. Now I know if I didn't have that drug habit I wouldn't be in this prison. It had got to the point that I really wasn't out there for nothing but just to do drugs.

And the following conversation with a thirty-year-old high-rate armed robber illustrates how a drug addiction propelled him to commit crimes.

Q: Why did you do it, at that time?
A: I was doing drugs real heavy, powerful drugs, and I liked it and by me liking that I took them chances. I really didn't think about the risks period then hardly. All I thought about was just getting dope and I'd go to any lengths to get it. The urge for that dope is stronger than getting caught so I'd go ahead and do it. I was doing it just to get money and it was for that damn dope. I didn't really think about all the trouble I'd end up in or anything. I was just wanting to get the money for dope.

Clearly, money for fifty-three of these participants represents the most significant motivating factor in their criminal calculus. Two-thirds needed money for either living expenses or miscellaneous expenses and considered crime a relatively easy way to maintain their lifestyles. A third, however, were driven to commit crimes because they needed money to regularly obtain physically addictive drugs (e.g., cocaine, heroin, and Dilaudid).[4]

A Sense of Accomplishment

A second and less-often-stated motivation for committing crimes was for the sense of accomplishment. From the respondents' self-reporting, this was the primary motivation only rarely. In fact, only three of the sixty reported "sense of accomplishment" rather than "easy money" as their motivation. The following dialogue with Floyd (a case study of Floyd appears in chapter 8), a high-rate shoplifter and later a high-rate armed robber, well illustrates this motivation in the case of shoplifting.

Q: Why would you do it?
A: Because I enjoyed it and the people with me enjoyed it. I'm the type of person, man, if I could steal something

from way in the back row or if the store manager is standing here and I could take something right under his nose, that's what I'd get.
Q: Why would you prefer that?
A: Because it was more of an accomplishment.

Although for some this motivation was primary, it nearly always was coupled with the desire for easily obtainable money or a sense of enjoyment, as the following comments from Floyd illustrate.

Q: What do you think the major motivations were to commit shoplifting?
A: Because it's easy money, it's exciting to do it, it ain't never hard to sell the stuff. But wanting to do it man, wanting to do it. Love to do it. *Love* to do it would be the word.

Those who committed crimes for the sense of accomplishment represent the segment that was very committed to a criminal lifestyle. They reported to me that crime was their job, their profession, and a way of obtaining both pecuniary and nonpecuniary benefits that they could not have earned from a "square-john" lifestyle. Although the sense of accomplishment was not a widespread motivational force among this sample, it did represent a significant factor in a few cases.

Crime as Sport

Two sample members reported in vivid detail a motivation for their crimes unlike those of others. Both individuals committed burglaries at a very high frequency and considered crime a fun and exciting game. The game-like rewards served as motivation to commit crimes. The easy money, which was motivating, paled in significance to beating the opponent of the game, or as they called it, "getting over on the law," which they considered a risky, yet psychologically fulfilling, act. I asked a twenty-nine-year-old, rather flamboyant, and very high-rate burglar why he committed the particular burglary he described to me. He described his motivation to commit burglaries in general.

> A: If I had to write a damn paper on the reason I steal, there would be one sentence—it was for the game. It's a high, now, I mean it's exhilarating. I mean, some people like racquetball and some people like tennis, but I get off going through doors.

Successfully completing a crime provided them with a sense of accomplishment and purpose, and reinforced their belief that they had "won the game." They functioned with the knowledge that in this game, like others, there emerges a winner and a loser. And whenever they were arrested and convicted, they simply admitted to having lost the game, but only temporarily.

The following dialogue with a twenty-eight-year-old high-rate offender clearly illustrates this motivation. This particular individual was a burglar who went on "burglary binges" much like drunks go on drinking binges. During those times he would burglarize nonstop in a rather blatant way, with the belief that he was untouchable. He fancied himself an outlaw, a modern day John Dillinger. Coming from a small town where law enforcement officers were few in number and lagged behind in investigative and detective skills, he considered himself beyond the law, as his willingness to boast about just how good he thought he was proves.

> A: It got to be a game. I've been locked up since I was sixteen. I've wasted the best years of my life. I can never get them back because I've played this game of "I'm going to beat them." And then you get to that stage, you wonder, "Who in the hell is it I'm trying to beat?" But it got to be a game. I played the game and lost. You got me. Let's go ahead and run it and start it over.
>
> Q: Did you feel like you were winning the game?
>
> A: Well, it starts, it's just like the trumpets at a horse race. I mean that sounds a silly way to sum it up, but now, that's the damn, that's just about it. It's like a starting gun at a swim meet that starts the game. And it's not ended until

you stand before that judge or you beat it. It's just like a chess game. I'm trying to stay a step ahead. I mean, fuck, it's a challenge. I mean, by God, it gets down to where it's just me against them and that's the way it is. To me, getting over on him or beating him at this game is 90 percent of it. The fucking money ain't nothing. Getting over on them is what it is. It got to where I just liked it.

Q: What did you like about it?

A: The excitement and the feeling of, you know, I fucked them, I mean, I had got over on them. They put their best investigators on me and I fucked them, man. I sit back and laugh thinking. Really. Basically, and you know yourself, it's a sorry mother-fucking thing, but I mean it provides that damn challenge. Crime was a game . . . with a whole lot of reality to it.

Thus, we can see from the two individuals who felt this motivation for committing crimes that the financial payoffs were rather insignificant compared to the psychologically fulfilling rewards of beating the opponent of the criminal game, a game with "a whole lot of reality to it." Ironically, they considered the years they spent incarcerated punishment for losing the game and not necessarily for breaking the law. One of the two individuals made the statement that going to prison was analogous to violating a rule in the board game *Monopoly*—go directly to jail, do not pass go, do not collect two hundred dollars. Again, this motivation was rare among this sample of repeat offenders but a very real factor in explaining why these few individuals committed crimes repetitively and what types of benefits they believed they would obtain from committing crimes.

Vengeance is Mine

The fourth type of motivation found among this sample, and only used by two armed robbers, was the desire for retaliation and vengeance. These armed robbers claimed to have suffered severely due to official governmental decision making, or lack of it. Both claimed to have lost legitimate earnings, both believed the government had done them an injustice, and one was homeless at the time that he committed his most serious crime of armed robbery. They acted criminally for revenge, generalizing and striking out at others as a representation of government and legitimate society. Although their crimes were individualistic, expressive acts and had no anti-systemic impact, they believed they were getting even with the status quo and the state that had caused them such harm.

Such motivation has been described by previous researchers. Becker, for example, wrote of revenge as both motivation and rationalization for committing crimes for individuals who believe they have been wronged and are entitled to such revenge. Revenge can also motivate individuals who believe their lives are out of control or that they are in the grips of "an uncontrollable force" (Becker, 1970: 332). Thus, individuals who commit crimes out of vengeance often define their situation as one imposed on them, over which they have little control.

The motivation of one of the two armed robbers clearly was shaped by his definition of his situation. He believed that some of his legal earnings from early in life had been wrongfully collected from him by the Internal Revenue Service. He claimed to have lost nearly all of his legally earned capital due to the collection of back taxes and legal fees. It was then that he decided to enter crime as a way of life to retaliate against the system and legitimate society. Crime as work also became a matter of principle to him since he had come to define legitimate work, where individual workers end up with little to show for their labor, as unfair. I had the following conversation with him about when he first began committing crimes in the early 1950s. He was fifty-eight years old and serving his third prison sentence.

Q: Did you try and find a job?
A: I was determined then that I wasn't going to work and make a living. I wasn't going to go out and work all day and week after week and pay the government for working. I mean this is the way I felt then. I felt that if I went out and got a job and they took federal tax out, they took

state tax out, they took medicare out, they took Social Security out and by the time I got my check they had already took out thirty dollars or forty dollars. So why would I work to pay the government for working? That's the way I felt.

The second armed robber expressed similar rebellion against a government that he believed had done him an injustice by refusing to assist him with his physical and emotional problems in a time of serious need. During the interview he certainly looked the part of a man in questionable health. He looked much older than his forty-two years, favored his bent back, and had some difficulty breathing. Although serving his third prison sentence, he claimed that he had committed relatively few crimes. He had committed the most serious, armed robbery, only twice and admitted he was motivated by frustration and a desire for vengeance. His words provide an inside view of his world.

A: The government did this somewhat to me too by denying me benefits.
Q: Your Social Security?
A: Yeah. I mean I was desperate. I didn't know what the hell I was going to do because I couldn't even keep the roof over my head. I moved into my car and I didn't have much of a car, but I slept in my car for a long time. I've had three back surgeries and now I've got heart trouble on top of the back surgery, so how in the hell am I going to get a job? My wife took me to _____ Mental Hospital because I did have an alcoholic problem and drugs and I asked her to take me there. And she did and I got turned away from over there, saying they didn't have the funds or money to help me and there was no room for me. No place for me there.
Q: And it was before that that you had gotten turned down for Social Security?
A: Right. I had many problems, mental problems. It got to the point where I knew I needed help and I couldn't get

it. And that whole chain of events got me right in prison. I was on my Social Security and they cut it out and when they cut it out it like to cut my life off. I lost my Social Security, I lost my truck and I didn't know what the hell I was going to do. I done it out of desperation and frustration at life, no help, no money, living in a car. I couldn't even take a bath. Nowhere to take a bath. I felt less than worthless.

Those who committed crimes out of vengeance calculated their crimes emotionally rather than logically, as the following comment from the fifty-eight-year-old robber illustrates.

A: When you're mad like that and a person did something to you, you be in a mental state of mind, you don't give a damn about no police, or being locked up, or a judge, or no damn nobody else.

This vengeance motivation was rare among this sample. These two individuals made their decisions and then committed their crimes using emotionally charged reasoning processes and modes of behavior. They were not that methodical in their planning, understandings of benefits and risks, or target selections. They typically robbed spontaneously and selected targets without rhyme or reason.

Crime as Power

A fifth and particularly important latent motivation found among armed robbers was the exertion of power and the control of victims and of the crime situation. The following conversation with a thirty-year-old, very experienced and seasoned armed robber illustrates how control and power were important elements to him, although money was obviously the primary benefit from the crime.

Q: Is that a pretty scary experience when you walk in with a gun pulled asking for money?

A: No, it's not really scary because you know you've got control of the situation, you know? It's a surprise, an element of surprise. You go in and you throw a gun on the table and everybody flips out. But it never did scare me because I always just put myself in their position. But it's just getting in that door. After you get through that door it ain't nothing, it's like you're running, like you own that place.

Q: You said like you own the place?

A: Yeah, you are ruling everything because everybody, whoever is in there is going to pay attention to you. I didn't want to hurt nobody. The only thing I wanted was the money. If you go in there you've got to play that act all the way out whether you get hurt or not.

Q: I think you're saying you were also prepared to do whatever to get the money?

A: Right. It wouldn't be that they'd try to harm me, it would be that they wouldn't give up the money. Because, you see, if you go in there and then let them tell you what to do, then there ain't no sense in you going in there at all.

Armed robbers who expressed this type of psychological benefit from and motivation for armed robbery were few in number (N=3). The armed robbers almost universally reported the desire for quick cash as the single motivating factor in their decisions to commit crime. And even the very few who reported this expressive benefit of power and control indicated that it was not as significant in motivating them as the desire or necessity of money.

Conclusion

Although the majority of these repetitive criminals reported one primary motivation, many reported one primary and other less important or latent motivations. But, not surprisingly, the goal-directed behavior among this sample was nearly entirely for monetary gain. The other motivational forces found among this group of chronic offenders pale in significance to money. Monetary gain, for whatever reason (e.g., for drugs, for living expenses, for pleasurable commodities) represents the most significant and most widely reported source of motivation among this sample of repetitive property criminals. The benefits that these offenders believed they would obtain by committing crimes was a significant component of the process of deciding to commit a crime.

Such findings from this sample of repetitive offenders are both similar and dissimilar to those from previous research. For example, this study differs from that of Frazier and Meisenhelder (1985), who reported that many of their ninety-five property offenders found crime to be exciting and believed they were "getting over on" someone or away with something. Many respondents in my sample reported the same. In fact, nearly all sixty found it exciting. But, excitement was a latent benefit neither primarily nor objectively sought after. Very few respondents reported excitement as a reason for committing crime. Rather, "quick, easy money" was the most common reason for doing crime. If committing crime was also exciting, then that added more pleasure to a financially rewarding activity. But, few entered crime motivated primarily by a desire for excitement.

These findings are similar to those of Reppetto (1974), who interviewed ninety-seven burglars and found money to be the primary benefit of crime. Excitement was mentioned most often among the young and least often among the old. This age-related difference is similar for the sixty men of my research. Motivation responses were measured across three different age periods of these men's lives.[5] These data show that excitement was often a primary motivator among the young, but its importance lessened with age until it typically became, at most, a latent benefit and motivating force.

In the next chapter, attention is given to the second analytical component of decision making—the alternative actions that these decision makers considered (i.e., those they defined as accessible) and that were available to them while they resolved their decision problems of committing or not committing crimes.

NOTES

1. The respondents typically would recall and begin to describe an exceptional crime that stood out in their minds for one reason or another. Knowing the types of crimes they committed and something about their frequency, I would remind them that I was interested in a typical crime that they had committed. They would then discontinue their description of the outstanding crime and begin describing a more typical crime for them. In this way, I was able to learn about the various events, conversations, and thoughts (as they reconstructed them) for a crime that they most frequently committed and the type most often committed by serious repetitive property criminals.

2. "High rate" as used in this work refers to those individuals in this sample who committed the most property crimes of the sixty. As an arbitrary cutoff point, high-rate criminals are those who committed more than one hundred property felonies during their lives in the "free world" and low-rate criminals, among this sample, are those who committed fewer than one hundred felony crimes during their lives in the "free world." These high-rate felons are classified as persistent decision makers, as mentioned in chapter 2 and explicated in chapter 8. High-rate criminals represent those criminals who are very committed to a criminal way of life and criminal profession. Such high-rate criminals clearly make decisions differently than low-rate repetitive criminals, who are classified as sporadic criminals in the taxonomy of decision makers among this sample.

3. "Getting over on" the law is a phrase used by criminals to describe successfully committing a crime and often refers to committing a crime with law enforcement officials nearby. "Getting over on" gives criminals satisfaction and is an expressive benefit derived from crime commission.

4. According to the *Physicians Desk Reference*, Dilaudid is a "hydrogenated ketone of morphine . . . a narcotic analgesic." The PDR has this to say about this widely used and very addictive drug:

> Small doses of Dilaudid produce effective and prompt relief of pain usually with minimal disturbance from nausea and vomiting. Generally, the analgesic action of Dilaudid is apparent within fifteen minutes and remains in effect for more than five hours. May be habit forming. The relative addiction potential does not exceed that of morphine with equi-analgesic doses (Physician's Desk Reference, 1977: 871).

Dilaudid was certainly a drug of choice among the very serious drug users and addicts among this sample. Dilaudid was preferred over heroin because the users claimed that they felt safe with Dilaudid, knowing that it was clean, laboratory produced and had not been "stepped on" (i.e., cut with an additive).

5. Each of the sixty was asked about motivation and benefit perceptions for three different age periods—juvenile (under age eighteen), young adult (ages eighteen to twenty-six), and adult (age twenty-seven and older). Their responses reveal that excitement as a motivational force and as a perceived benefit lessened with age.

4 Alternatives to Crime Commission

> Freedom slipped away from me at twenty-three
> I broke the lock on one too many door,
> My hungry hands would not behave
> When they wrapped around the things they craved,
> I just got tired of being poor.
> —Dallas Frazier, "I Just Got Tired of Being Poor"

Decision-making researchers, guided by rational choice theory, recently have indicated that an important component of theoretical decision making—alternatives considered by the decision maker—have gone uninvestigated. To further understand criminal decision-making, investigators point to the need for specific information on offenders' perceptions of their legitimate opportunities for getting money (e.g., Feeney, 1986). These perceptions are shaped by more than the individual's own subjectivity. They are shaped by their objective material circumstances. Researchers of crime displacement also address this issue, since criminals who are displaced from committing a particular crime may not consider legal alternatives as potential options and may simply choose another crime as an alternative to the original crime. For example, Feeney (1986) reports that in his sample, armed robbers usually considered an illegal alternative to robbery rather than a legal option.

In the next few pages, I describe both the legitimate and illegitimate alternatives available to and considered by this sample of repetitive property offenders. Their explanations offer insight into an important dimension of criminal decision making.

Legitimate Alternatives

Previous research indicates that criminals often have legitimate jobs (e.g., Akerstrom, 1985). But crime, as work, provides them with both instrumental (i.e., pecuniary) and expressive (i.e., non-pecuniary) rewards that their legitimate jobs did not provide; for example, "quick, easy money," psychological fulfillment, and a sense of accomplishment or usefulness. Holzman (1983) found that 85 percent of his sample of criminals had full-time jobs at the time of their arrests. But they moonlighted in illegal occupations and envisioned themselves as entrepreneurs who someday would be legitimately self-employed. These findings from previous research indicate that other respondents have had legitimate alternatives, such as work, available to them.

Two related points emerged from this study, one of which is vastly different from that of Holzman's. First, nearly all of these participants were not employed full-time at the time of their arrests and most were either unemployed or underemployed.[1] Their objective economic conditions are important for understanding the alternatives available to and considered by them when resolving criminal decision problems. Rather than focusing on individual differences among Holzman's (1983) sample and mine, other explanations may be found in structural changes that have occurred within the domestic labor market during the past decade. The labor market has tightened and employers can now demand from employees more education, specialization, computer skills, and stable work experience than ever before. The labor market has become a buyer's market. Just as fifteenth century peasants were marginalized by a change in production processes, individuals in our society with few job skills and little education increasingly have been displaced and have lost what little stake in conformity they might have had. The following dialogue with a thirty-eight-year-old prisoner who committed burglaries and armed robberies but who specialized in shoplifting, is illustrative.

Q: Did you see any alternatives at all, like did you think you had a chance at a job?

A: Yeah, but jobs were hard to find, especially for a young man that didn't have no education and been in trouble.

And a thirty-year-old armed robber reported similarly:

Q: Did you see any alternatives to committing robbery?
A: I tried [to find a job]. The moment you said you was put in jail or a reference to something like that, you was out.

Legitimate opportunities for the majority of these respondents to earn a decent wage were structurally limited. Although they may not have been able to articulate it, they were aware, at least intuitively, of the odds against them, and often opted for illegitimate means to obtain socially approved success goals (Merton, 1949; Cloward and Ohlin, 1960; Gordon, 1973). The majority had "everything going against them," that is, most had dropped out of school or were dismissed at a young age and were unable to develop marketable job skills. Thus, when they did work, it was nearly always in menial jobs and jobs that they held for short periods of time (as transient workers, they frequently moved from one job to another). All sixty had been in prison at least one time before and after their first incarceration found themselves labeled and stigmatized as "ex-cons." They then experienced those well-known difficulties associated with being ex-convicts (Goffman, 1963; Becker, 1963). The following conversation with a thirty-four-year-old burglar about his employment after his first incarceration typifies this experience among these men.

Q: Did you see any other alternatives to committing robbery, like a job? Did you think you could find a job?
A: I tried to find one. But, when you commit the crime, you commit it and you get sentenced to pay a debt to society. But that debt's never paid. You cannot pay that debt. You're screwed the rest of your life.

A second and similar finding to Holzman's (1983), is that typically many of the sixty envisioned themselves as entrepreneurs, innovative ones to be sure (given that their business is illegal), who dreamed of one day owning their own businesses. They had a desire to apply the skills they possessed (e.g., coolness and nerve) to a legitimate autonomous job. The comments of the following criminal, a thirty-three-year-old, formerly drug-addicted individual who committed forgeries at a very high rate are typical for this sample.

> A: I'm going to live out my fantasy or whatever it is, you know, about getting this house and building me a business of my own, you know. I want to be the boss.[2]

Dreams of self-employment offer them the hope of earning a decent legitimate wage and exercising their nerve. This, they believe, would provide them autonomy, which would allow them to create and revise the rules guiding their own work and to become what most working people desire, "masters of their own environment" (Terkel, 1972; Braverman, 1974; Gordon et al., 1982). These projections are representative of their often distorted perceptions of the objective legitimate options available to them. The following conversation with a thirty-year-old high-rate burglar whose father was self-employed and who grew up in an upper-middle class family in a small town is illustrative of the distorted preceptions that he and others like him held about their possibilities of becoming self-employed.

> Q: Do you think being locked up will have a negative impact on your trying to find a job?
> A: Probably not because I'm going to be self-employed. I'll probably get a grocery store with a little gas station hooked to it and sell beer. And with a little luck a *Stop and Go* or something. I have a good business mind.

Most of these men have lived on legitimate earnings very infrequently during their lives. But, after having served two or more incarcerations, they believed they would be able to survive and be somewhat content on legitimate earnings. This belief is indicative of both their hope and their distorted perceptions of their objective legitimate options. They typically had no idea that they might be destined to reap subsistence wages and little knowledge about the type of lifestyle that such earnings determine. Their distorted beliefs were supported by the fact that they had lived somewhat comfortably in prison on their prison earnings and believed that they certainly could live as comfortably in the "free world." They failed to consider that they had almost no living expenses while incarcerated. The following comment from a thirty-year-old armed robber who rarely had been employed illustrates this finding.

> A: I see if I can work in [prison] making forty or fifty dollars a month and can survive and live off of that, then I won't have no problem going out in society working if it's nothing but minimum wages.

Doubtless, education, job skills, work experience and a clean record provide individuals with legitimate opportunities (i.e., they provide social status, mobility, and economic stability). Lacking these particular assets in their lives, the respondents innovated by replacing legitimate means to obtaining and owning socially approved material possessions with illegitimate means. Similar patterns that have been uncovered in recent research suggest that "social conditions . . . may limit opportunity and reduce an individual's investment in society, leading to both drug abuse and criminal behavior" (Innes, 1988: 2). Table 4.1 illustrates the alternatives considered by this sample.

Working for a Living

Legitimate employment certainly was considered an alternative to crime at some point during these men's lives. But, unlike a few naive respondents mentioned earlier, most were aware, at one time or another, of the meager wages they were destined to reap, the difficult jobs they would have to work, and the conditions under which they would be forced to labor. Again, the words of the thirty-year-old from the upper-middle class family reinforce this theme.

Table 4.1   Alternatives Considered

Alternatives Considered	Number	Percent
No alternative considered	43	72
Another crime	4	6
Legitimate employment	4	6
Borrowing money	3	5
Rejection of work ethic	6	10

Totals may not equal 100 due to rounding

> Q: At that time you said you were out of work and you took this [gun] running job. Did you see any other alternatives that you could have chosen?
> A: Not unless I wanted to go to work in the coal mines with my wife's cousins. I couldn't see myself coming out of a coal mine at four o'clock in the afternoon, black sooted face.

They did not consciously think of working each time they confronted a criminal decision problem. In fact, only two offenders reported seeking legitimate work while resolving the specific criminal decision problem that I questioned them about. Another two reported that before their most intensive periods of crime commission, they had sought legitimate work, but to no avail. The majority previously had appraised working for a wage and had rejected that option due to one or more of the following three reasons. First, they were unable to secure employment.

> A: Nobody would hire me. Employment was impossible so I started robbing.

Second, they were aware of the limitations that a legitimate wage from a menial job would afford.

> A: I had seen the way my father was getting the things that he had in life. But, I just wanted things then and there. Like a new car, I couldn't see myself working for two years saving money and then going out and putting it on a car. I wanted my car then and there.

A: I figured shoot, why go out and work when a man can go out here and do this right here and make a whole lot of money just in a little bit.

Third, as part of their own identity and presentation of themselves, they simply refused to work a legitimate job for a living. A few high-frequency participants made a conscious decision to not work a legitimate job and instead to support themselves with illegal earnings. These individuals typically had few expenses (since they refused to buy cars, electronic equipment, and furniture the way most people do) and shunned investing in a legitimate lifestyle. The following dialogue with a forty-year-old high-rate burglar illustrates the point.

Q: You didn't used to work, did you?
A: Not at all. I wouldn't work if you asked me to work. I thought it was other ways to do things besides working. I thought you were a fool to work. "Why should you work you fool? You ain't never going to have nothing." That's what I used to say.
Q: How about picking up an odd job for half a day?
A: No-o-o. I thought I was too cool, too cool man. I thought I was too good. That would have been against my dignity to try to work. I wouldn't want nobody to know that I was doing that.

While legitimate work was not a viable option for some of these individuals, an often volunteered comment was that the benefits derived from illegal adventures dwarfed those derived from working. The material benefits were especially meaningful given the ease with which they were obtained. For example, I posed the following question to a former drug-addicted high-rate criminal who, unlike the majority of offenders, committed a wide array of crimes as divergent as armed robbery and forgery.

Q: Why did you do the forgery . . . at that time?
A: I didn't want to work and forgery was pretty much the easiest thing.

When I asked the following question of a thirty-seven-year-old burglar, he described how working, even for more than subsistence wages, did not compare to the benefits from criminal enterprises.

> Q: Did you see any alternatives that you could have taken instead of breaking into houses and stealing boats and tractors?
>
> A: This lady I was living with, she had a girl friend . . . [who] owned a big old trailer park. And she . . . told me, "I'll give you five hundred dollars a week to come up here and run it for me, to keep the maintenance up." But, shit, I was done into burglaries so bad, man, that I wasn't about to give up an easy damn job like that to go out and actually work.

And the following dialogue with a twenty-eight-year-old who had committed a large number of armed robberies and had never worked a legitimate job illustrates the appealing qualities of crime over working for a living. He too describes how easily money is made from crime, compared to legitimate earnings.

> Q: Did you, at that time, think of any alternative to doing the armed robbery?
>
> A: At the time I really didn't like working because the life I was living, the money that I was getting was way more easy than going out and working for it.

The following dialogue with a burglar who specialized in stealing kitchen appliances from newly built, vacant apartment complexes shows how his earnings from crime were much more lucrative than those that he could have expected from working a legitimate job.

> Q: Did you think of anything else you could do for money, at that time?
>
> A: Well, it's not every day you can go out in an hour's time and make five hundred to one thousand dollars, you know. There's just no job in the world that pays that, and

even if you didn't make but two hundred or three hundred, that's more than you could make in a week. And say for an hour's work, you take off all week and not worry about working no more.

At that time in their lives, these respondents believed that employment, if secured, would provide them with less than fulfilling wages and psychological rewards. Based on their experiences in the legitimate work world, they related to me that legitimate work, if obtainable, would offer only subsistence wages. Also, in a restrictive, controlled work place, there would be no room for the skills they had developed (e.g., cool, nerve, and network connections). They typically believed that legitimate work failed to offer not only autonomy but also satisfaction. The following conversation with a twenty-nine-year-old very high-rate burglar who fancied himself a genuine outlaw illustrates how he received psychologically fulfilling payoffs from doing burglaries.

Q: Does work bore you, legitimate work?
A: Yeah. If I can't get something that keeps my mind working and keeps me going I can't . . . I ain't got that good a damn mind, but I mean I've got to keep busy.
Q: And burglary does that for you?
A: Oh, hell yeah. I was having too good a time. I thought, "This is fun. Hell, the whole town is mine."

Given the limitations on their legitimate work possibilities, they were unable to (1) obtain employment or (2) obtain employment that paid them more than a subsistence wage. Their exclusion from the labor force may indeed result from constrictive changes in the labor market and the growing demands for would-be employees to possess certain skills, legitimate employment histories, and legitimate lifestyles.

Such findings from this sample are supported by recent data from the National Institute of Justice. Their estimates are that at least 40 percent of all prisoners were unemployed at the time of their arrest and of the 60 percent who were employed, 12 percent held only part-time jobs. The Justice Department concluded from their research that "the highest incarceration rate among U.S. males age sixteen to sixty-four was among those who were unemployed" (U.S. Department of Justice, 1983: 38). NIJ also reports that the typical inmate was living below the poverty level at the time of his arrest and almost half of those reported annual legitimate incomes of less than three thousand dollars. A more recent study indicates that 56 percent of men incarcerated were unemployed at the time of their arrest (Austin and Irwin, 1990). These recent findings indicate that our state prisons hold members of the underclass or, in Marxian terms, the "lumpen proletariat," the chronically unemployed and underemployed.

Borrowing Money as a Legitimate Alternative

Given the constraints on their securing and maintaining legitimate work, the most typical legitimate alternative considered by this sample was an attempt to borrow money from relatives and friends. Although this alternative is the most typical, of the sixty, only three attempted to borrow money prior to deciding to commit the crime that they recounted in detail to me. But, this low number is to be expected, for borrowing money is not a real solution to their need for money. After all, criminals do not commit crimes because they temporarily need money. Borrowing money is a temporary solution while working—whether legally or illegally—is a continuing solution to the necessity of money. Also, this legitimate alternative is one that requires minimal initiative and investment of time and is certainly in line with a thief's normal attempts to obtain money, with little initiative and investment of time. The following conversation with a twenty-eight-year-old, high-rate burglar formerly addicted to cocaine shows how his attempts to borrow money were futile.

> Q: Did you consider doing anything else for money, at that time?
> A: I went to the bank four different times. I went to four or five different loan companies, you know, the ones that say, "Come on in and borrow money on your word" and

all this. That's a crock of shit. They ain't anybody going to lend you nothing. I mean, it's there for the taking, but it ain't there for the loaning.

Although some related that they had successfully borrowed money at one time or another, they also realized they could not continually rely on that option, as the following comments from a forty-six-year-old burglar serving his fifth prison sentence show.

Q: Did you think of anything else that you could do to get money, like borrow it?
A: No, I'd done run that in the ground, see. You burn that up, that's burned up right there, borrowing.

For some who previously had relied on borrowing money to support themselves, the well had run dry, so to speak, and they were unable to borrow more. The desperation to borrow money is evident in the words of this thirty-eight-year-old burglar serving his second prison sentence.

Q: You said you tried other ways to get money. Like what?
A: I had went to my sister's house to get some money. I went to ask her to let me have some money and she said at that particular time she couldn't. I asked my sister but I couldn't convince her to let me have the money.

Thus, borrowing from family or friends was a temporary alternative to crime for some of these men. Only three reported that they attempted to borrow prior to committing the crime they described to me. They realized borrowing was a short-term solution to ongoing money problems.

Drug Addiction and Alternatives

The majority of these sixty respondents had less than a high school education, had developed no job skills, had not established a stable and durable record of employment, had a criminal record, and several were severely addicted to drugs or alcohol. These addicted individuals had almost no alternatives available to them to support their habits besides crime, other than to fundamentally alter their lifestyles (e.g., to simply "just say no" to drugs).

Recently the Bureau of Justice surveyed 27,000 state prisoners sentenced for property crimes and found that 40 percent, while committing crimes, were under the influence of a drug (Innes, 1988). This figure includes those individuals who were addicted to a drug and those individuals who used drugs as a neutralization technique to commit the risky decision and action (described in chapter 5). Just as national data show, seventeen of these sixty were severely addicted to drugs to the point that they could not maintain a regular full-time job.[3] They reported that they committed crimes to purchase the drugs to which they were addicted. They knew that crime, unlike other alternatives, would be a monetarily rewarding and rational way to obtain what they needed. I asked an armed robber about his reasons for choosing crime over another course of action. He answered the following:

> A: I knew [crime] was wrong, but like I say, man, it was wrong in the eyes of the beholder. You know? I mean, I'm needing a shot of dope, it's not wrong for me to go get it. I have to get it, however I can. To me it wasn't wrong. I had to have it and I had to get it from somewhere.

The following dialogue with another high-rate offender who reported that his drug use had propelled him to commit crimes illustrates how drug addiction contributes to criminal involvement.

> Q: How did your drug use contribute to committing crimes?
> A: Whenever you get hooked on cocaine, man, you'll do anything in the world for it. Whatever you need to do is what you'll do.

A thirty-year-old prisoner who had committed a wide array of property crimes answered in a way that indicates that drug addiction was the fundamental reason for his committing crimes.

He and others like him were fully aware that not only could they not find any job, but also that a legitimate job with a salary they realistically could have earned would not have offered them enough money to support their serious habits.

A: I tried to stay away from crime, other than selling cocaine. I was determined not to rob any more and when my cocaine sales did not contribute enough to my cocaine consumption, then it became necessary that I rob. Nobody would hire me. I was an ex-con and I tried, I really tried to get gainful employment. There was nobody looking to hire me with my record. I went in as a juvenile and came out as an adult and didn't have any legitimate employment resume to submit. Employment was impossible. So, I started robbing.

And the same sentiment is expressed in the following:

Q: Did you ever see another way to get money other than crime?
A: There was no other way to support a drug habit and the best way, the fastest way was stealing. I mean, there was always something to steal. All I had to do was look for it and it was always something to steal somewheres.

These offenders knew that crime would be a monetarily rewarding and "rational" means to obtain what they needed. Social theorists and researchers for years have written of the various modes that individuals use to obtain socially acceptable indicators of success and for these drug-addicted, crime was a way to meet socially unacceptable needs (e.g., Merton, 1949; Gordon, 1973). By situating these offenders' explanations and objective conditions within this tradition, it becomes apparent how these addicts defined their situations as such that it became necessary to pursue illegitimate means to obtain physical necessities—physically addicting drugs.

Given the objective conditions of nearly all sixty interviewees, their legitimate alternatives were very limited in scope and number. The average educational level for this sample was tenth grade. Few had developed marketable employment skills, they had records of criminal involvement, and many had drug and alcohol dependencies. Thus, they were excluded from participating in legitimate alternatives given that they had so few available to them. And when faced with a decision to commit a crime, it was only logical to give legitimate alternatives little consideration and weight.

Illegitimate Alternatives

Previous research suggests that criminals typically think only of illegal alternatives before committing a crime (e.g., Cornish and Clarke, 1987). Of those in my sample who actually considered an alternative to the crime that they eventually committed, the majority reported likewise. Consider the following words of a twenty-eight-year-old low-rate armed robber.

> Q: Did you think of other ways of making money?
> A: Well, every now and then I might run across something that I could get right spur-of-the-moment. But mainly I stayed with robbery.
> Q: Are you talking about legal or illegal things?
> A: Illegal.

But, nearly all related that even when they considered another illegal act, they did not want to change their modus operandi or specialty at that particular juncture in their careers. Most reported considering another crime of the same type that they were thinking of committing, that they normally committed, and that they felt adept at. The following two individuals, high-rate armed robbers, indicate that they had no desire to change their specialty and do anything other than armed robbery.

> Q: Did you consider doing anything else?
> A: I mostly did armed robbery. Reason why, because that was the quick and easiest way of getting money. Cause if you do a burglary then whatever you get you have to sell it or you've got to find somebody to buy. But, if you do armed robbery, it's money right there.

Alternatives to Crime Commission

Q: At that time, did you consider doing anything else besides the robbery?

A: I'm thinking, well, in a burglary, if I go break in something I've got to turn around and sell it, whereas if I rob these people, I've got the money right then.

While resolving the decision problem of committing or not committing a crime, the majority considered only the type of crime they were committing regularly at that particular period of their careers and most had a specific target in mind. The decision, then, was not one that involved sophisticated calculations of their criminal specialities compared to illegal alternatives and the perceived benefits from each. Rather, the criminals had some general ideas about the alternatives available to them but did not consider them viable due to their limited knowledge about the specifics of each alternative. Some made quick and simple comparisons between their criminal speciality and another crime, but the vast majority plodded right along and committed the criminal act with no thoughts of doing anything other than that particular crime.

In fact, forty-three of the sixty reported that they did not consider any alternative to the crime that they committed. The following words from a thirty-year-old armed robber about his early criminal activity illustrates this very common pattern.

Q: Did you ever talk about doing anything else to get the money or did that ever enter the conversation?

A: No, that never came up . . . we never did talk about going and looking at this, finding a job. It was always taking something and it never crossed our mind, you know, why don't we go and check out this job, this and that. That wasn't even—well, it wasn't on my mind and didn't none of the rest of them ever bring up the conversation.

And the words of a high-rate shoplifting specialist:

Q: Did you see any alternatives to the shoplifting that you were doing at that time?

A: Never looked for none because there wasn't anything that I enjoyed more than shoplifting.

The following words of a drug-addicted burglar serving his second prison sentence well illustrate this point.

Q: Did you think about any alternatives to make money that day [the day of the burglary]?
A: Oh, besides breaking in there?
Q: Yeah.
A: No, that's the only one I, that's all I knew at the time.

This lack of alternative actions being contemplated is a reflection of their often limited objective circumstances, since few had alternatives available to them. Not contemplating alternatives is also in line with the principle of immediate utility, which states that a "course of conduct is the right one . . . if and only if it is the best alternative under the circumstances; and the best alternative is the one that has the best overall consequences" (Hill et al., 1979: 48). These criminals knew that the crime they could perform well would bring them the best overall consequences.

Conclusion

Given their objective circumstances and their limited knowledge about legitimate and illegitimate alternatives many of these offenders, especially the severely drug-addicted and the chronically unemployed, may have chosen the best alternative available to them since crime often allowed them to obtain satisfaction of their immediate needs. Recent examinations of alternatives available to repetitive criminals yields similar results as research on the class content among state prison inmates. In the first, there are almost no alternatives available; and in the second, the class content is disproportionately skewed toward the lower class. Both findings are indicative of their class positions.[4]

This research supports the assumption that objective conditions strongly influence perceptions. The offenders' criminal calculus included little assessment of alternatives since their circumstances disallowed their pursuit of any realistic alternatives.

On one hand, since numerous alternatives were not evaluated during the decision-problem resolution, it appears that the steps of "rational decision making" were not fully exhausted, making their decision making far from rational. But, on the other hand, given their backgrounds and objective circumstances, and their subjective interpretations of their circumstances, their decision making appears logical if it is placed within the psychology of "situational rationality," where the individual's own subjective appraisal and objective needs and ways of meeting those needs are limited and hence evaluated situationally (Ehrlich, 1973; Gordon, 1973). Given their needs and the limitations of meeting them, their actions, including ignoring other alternatives, appear somewhat logical, especially because the majority thought they would not get caught and believed that if they were caught the punishment would be minimal (see chapter 6 for an explanation of these dimensions of their criminal calculus). The point is, they still may have been acting in a logical fashion, even though they did not consciously think of alternatives to their specific crime.

Crime appears to have been a rational response for most of these criminals—a response to the appeal of success goals offered as desirable and obtainable by this society; goals that individuals with legitimate lifestyles often desire and can affordably obtain. These criminals believed there was no better method of obtaining money and possessions than illegal actions. Ironically, despite the rational calculation of how to get the most money in the easiest way, shortly after committing a crime they usually had little money or commodities to show for their efforts. They typically blew the money on drugs and easily consumable commodities. The "easy money" most reported was also easy to spend. All participants reported that illegally obtained money "spent faster" than legally obtained, and that for them, the old adage, "easy come, easy go," has a ring of truth to it. So they had little to show for their risky ventures and labors.

It became clear while interviewing the sample members that they possessed less than optimal knowledge about legitimate alternatives. Although some considered legitimate alternatives to crime, those who did had little information and knowledge about them. The criminal decision-problem resolution, as with most decision problems, clearly was reduced to their subjective evaluation. They defined their decision as a rational one, which suggests that rational decision-making is a fundamentally subjective process.

NOTES

1. "Underemployed" here is reserved for those individuals whose jobs disallow their working as many hours as they need to or want to. A growing segment of the labor force is finding itself employed only part-time and increasingly in low-paying service-related jobs and therefore, underemployed (U.S. Department of Labor, 1988).

2. As an aside, it is interesting that being a crook and being a boss are so related. This similarity would probably come as no surprise to the millions of working class men and women of this country, who fear both street criminals and their bosses, wouldn't invite either over for dinner, and perceive both as hedonists.

3. Perhaps more surprising, eighteen of the sixty admittedly experienced chronic alcohol-related problems (e.g., alcohol interfering with personal relationships).

4. For a more detailed explanation of these criminals' class positions and their exclusion from the labor force, see Tunnell, 1990b.

Neutralizing Fears During Criminal Decision Making 5

> Look here now buddy, say you wanna be like me,
> Pull out your six shooter and rob every bank you can see,
> Tell the judge I said it was alright.
> —Bob Dylan, "Bob Dylan's Blues"

During the course of this research, I realized that these repeat property offenders often decided to commit crimes with the aid of one or more neutralization techniques that enabled them to decide to commit crimes in a seemingly less-than-rational manner. The offenders either consciously or subconsciously used these techniques. This general finding is in line with the seminal work of Sykes and Matza (1957) that describes neutralization techniques and their use among delinquents, primarily subconsciously but also consciously to neutralize the guilt associated with doing crime. Although this sample of sixty property offenders relied on neutralization techniques, they did not necessarily use them to neutralize guilt. Rather, they used them before committing crimes to neutralize their apprehensions, fears, and worries as they made decisions to commit crimes.

Altered States

The first technique of neutralization identified among this sample was also the most commonly used—drugs and alcohol. Respondents nearly always described their typical perceptions of risk as feelings similar to "butterflies" rather than as perceptions or understandings of real consequences that might befall them because of their criminal activities. The use of alcohol and drugs helped alleviate their butterflies during both the decision and the crime. This technique enabled them to overcome nervousness and engage in a risky decision and event that they reportedly could not have done otherwise, as the following dialogue with a veteran of numerous armed robberies illustrates.

> A: So I was always kind of nervous unless I had done drunk a few beers or smoked some weed to build my nerves up.
> Q: Drinking and smoking. Is that something that you typically did before pulling off a robbery?
> A: Yeah. I needed something to build my nerves up, to relax me, stop me from shaking. If I'm a little intoxicated, I'm ready for it, whatever goes down.

The majority of those who relied on this technique had some idea that they wanted to commit a crime before they began indulging in alcohol or drugs, as was also found by Petersilia et al. (1978). They often *first* rudimentarily decided to commit the crime and then drank or did drugs for courage to complete the decision and risky act. The following dialogue with a residential burglar demonstrates how he used alcohol to facilitate an act that he wanted to do, but seemingly could not without the help of booze.

> A: See, I wanted to do that burglary anyway before I started drinking, but I didn't have no help. So, what I'd do is I'd get me some help. I called it false courage. Because that's the courage that I need and I've never been one to do anything without false courage.
> Q: What happens to your courage when you start drinking?
> A: Alcohol gives me more strength to do stuff like that. I would always be drinking when I would do that stuff. It would always kind of boost me up and build my hopes up that I could do it. Because when you get to drinking, you drink so much and you get so drunk or something or another like that, you'll do anything.

Table 5.1 Neutralization Techniques Used

Neutralization Technique	Number	Percent
Alcohol and drugs	41	68
Conversation with others	16	27
Influence of older individuals	54	90
Putting risks out of mind	38	63

The total number is greater than the N of 60 and the total percent is greater than 100 due to some overlap among the sample members' reporting.

Forty-one of the sixty (68 percent) claimed to always need the help of drugs or alcohol before committing their crimes. The potential risk of their actions was deadened by the "buzz." This discovery is similar to that found by Petersilia et al. (1978) in that 60 percent of that sample was under the influence of alcohol or a drug at the time they committed the property crime for which they were arrested. And more recently, the federal government reported from survey research with 27,000 state prisoners that 40 percent of those serving time for property crimes were under the influence of a drug when they committed their crimes (Innes, 1988). This figure includes both those with addictions and those who used drugs as a neutralization technique. Table 5.1 illustrates the various neutralization techniques used among this sample.

One armed robber among this sample explained his use of alcohol in this way:

> A: I would get kind of buzzy before I would do it because you get ready to do something and you're straight, man, you'll be having butterflies. If you're up there buzzing you're going to have a little butterfly but after you get in there and get situated, well, then it's a piece of cake. You're ruling everything.

And another robber explained it similarly:

> A: I can't sit here and think of a time that I went in and pulled an armed robbery when I was straight. Maybe I'd smoke a joint or something and sometimes I was drunk, but I always had a little buzz when I went in.

Not only armed robbers who committed very risky actions relied on the deadening effects of alcohol and drugs, but also those who committed actions with less risk and with less potential for violent confrontations depended on the deadening effect of alcohol and drugs. The following dialogue with a burglar illustrates how a "buzz" enabled him to indulge in the risky decision and venture.

> Q: Usually are you straight or high when you break into a place?
> A: I like to have a buzz. It calms you down a little bit. To build your, to give you the courage, not just to build your courage up. Just to give it to you, give you that, knock the edge off.

The use of alcohol and drugs enabled them to engage in both risky decisions and actions that they claimed to want to do but could not have done without neutralizing their anxieties. This neutralization technique, which was the most widely used ongoing technique among this sample, reduced their internal queasiness about the decision they faced.

Talking it Up

The second technique of neutralization identified was the calming effect of conversations with cohorts while the decision to commit a crime was made. Social psychologists inform us that one way to reduce fear or anxiety prior to engaging in a risky decision or event is to become engrossed in an absorbing activity, such as conversation with others (e.g., Lee, 1971; Hill et al., 1979; Gardner, 1985). Such action reinforces the risky behavior until it is completed (i.e., until the decision to commit the crime has been made). Conversation used in this way is a fear-neutralization technique.

Conversation among criminal cohorts included discussions of the logistics of the particular crime they were contemplating and allowed for encouragement that helped convince them to participate in it. Cohorts often recounted previous successful crimes as a means of encouraging each other. This technique is similar to that used in organized athletics, where team members recount past victories prior to meeting an opponent as a way of "psyching" each other up or encouraging each other to believe they will be successful in the event facing them. The following conversation with a very active residential burglar illustrates this point.

Q: So did you all talk about other things besides the specific plan?
A: Yeah, old burglaries, you know, like, "Remember the one at so and so we did last week," or something like that.

Conversation before the crime, however, was usually one-sided, as the individuals only discussed the anticipated benefits of their actions rather than discussing both the anticipated benefits and possible risks. As a result, the use of this neutralization technique among this sample seemingly impeded rational calculation. According to the burglar in the following dialogue, he and his cohorts talked of the positive rewards from doing a particular burglary.

Q: Well, as you all rode around and drank and smoked that day thinking about doing the crime, what kinds of things did you all talk about?
A: We talked about when we got all that money that they said that man had. We talked about, "Oh, we would do this and do that with that money." We was going to go and buy some nice cars and make us some hot rods and stuff out of them and build them up and make them mean and stuff.

Another burglar reports similarly:

Q: Tell me what kinds of things were talked about or what kinds of things you thought about.
A: Thought it would be easy, and what we'd make. How much money we'd make and what we'd get. How much we'd make off of it.

Q: What kinds of things were you thinking in your own mind, that maybe you all didn't talk about?
A: I was thinking about the big lick [i.e., big money].

This neutralization technique was used by sixteen of the sample members (27 percent) and nearly always among those who committed crimes with others. Their belief in strength in numbers enabled them to neutralize their fears. While assessing the decision problems and possible outcomes, their calculations were one-sided because only the benefits were thought of and discussed. Similar findings have emerged in earlier research (e.g., Peterson et al., 1980).

Higher Loyalties

The third technique of neutralization identified was the influence that older individuals had on these men's lives. Nearly all of the respondents reported they started committing crimes at a young age and were strongly encouraged or influenced by an older individual who already was involved in crime and who therefore was viewed as more knowledgeable about risky decisions and actions. In fact fifty-four of the sixty (90 percent) reported being deferential to an older criminal at some point during their criminal careers.

A: I always wanted to hang around the older guys and the guys that I hung around with was older. They was into drugs. In order for me to be in with the crowd, I always like to hang around older people.
Q: Were they into burglaries too?
A: Yeah, they was into some of everything. The things that I seen them do, I liked it and I wanted to do it myself because I thought it was a big thing. If you did that you was cool and all that.

They typically related to me that the older individual would point to his success at committing crimes and promise that they, younger inexperienced individuals, with his assistance and expertise, could do likewise. The younger and not yet successful criminals would then defer to the older criminals' expertise, as the following dialogue with an individual who consistently relied on the leadership of his older brother illustrates.

> A: I was scared. I said, "I'll tell you what," I said, "we may get in trouble or we might end up getting killed by doing this," because I hadn't never did nothing like that. But he said, "No, everything will be alright." Said, "You ain't got nothing to worry about." So, I kindly figured to myself, well, I guess maybe it will be alright.
> Q: So, why did you think it would be?
> A: Because he had got out of a lot of stuff and he had did a lot of stuff and had never got caught at it. I figured well, if he can get by with all them things, I know we can get by with just this one thing.

They believed that the older/wiser person already had considered the potential risks and benefits of crime and had calculated correctly. They relied on the other criminal to do the thinking so that they did not have to consider the rationality or potential risks of their actions. As a result, their anxieties were neutralized (Sykes and Matza, 1957).

Not only did they rely on the older individual to make decisions about risky criminal events, but they also relied on the older person's authority in commandeering the actual risky event—the crime. One participant in particular who committed a great number of crimes throughout his life was asked if he armed himself while doing house burglaries.

> A: We always had a handgun on every burglary that we done.
> Q: You carried a gun?
> A: I never did carry one but mostly the oldest person in the group always had the gun and he would be the one that looked out, made sure everything was okay.

The influence of the older and more experienced individual facilitated decisions to commit crimes, especially those early crimes. Nearly all sixty had their decision making influenced by an older/wiser individual early in life. Those in the sample who committed the fewest number of crimes throughout their lives (i.e., the sporadic or low-rate offenders) continued to rely on the expertise of the older/wiser individual.

This shows that individuals who engage in crime are able to neutralize negative feelings by being loyal to individuals in positions of illegitimate authority. The compatibility found within primary groups contributed to the influence on the younger offenders by older individuals who occupied positions of leadership, respect, and authority within the deviant subculture of their group (Akers, 1977). Those men who continued to rely on the leadership of older individuals throughout their lives of criminal involvement likewise continued to defer to the more knowledgeable authority. Although fifty-four of the respondents reported that at some time during their criminal activity they relied on the expertise of an older and wiser individual, the vast majority relied on such expertise early in life. Thus, this neutralization technique was not an ongoing factor in the maintenance of their criminal careers. Rather, the dependence on the older offender and his knowledge occurred at a time when their involvement with crime was first initiated. The majority used this technique of neutralization early in life as a way of initiating involvement in crime commission and at some point, as they aged, came to rely less and less on the authority of the older/wiser individual.

Out of Mind

The fourth technique of neutralization that I identified was the ability to put all thoughts of potential negative consequences out of their minds. They simply refused to think about possible formal and informal sanctions that might result from their actions. A persistent residential burglar related to me the way that he cognitively managed to avoid thoughts of risk.

Q: So what negative things did you think about?
A: At the time you block out all those thoughts . . . you've got to have the money and when you get the money then

you'll worry after that. It's just something you do. You block it all out because you know it's wrong. It's just a temporary block.

The few participants who did minimally worry about risks prior to doing the crime managed to put those concerns and worries out of their minds while actually doing the crime (Cressey, 1973). An armed robber explained how he managed to rid himself of worries.

> A: When I walked in the place I really didn't think nothing. I mean it was just like my mind was blank when I walked in. I knowed what I was in there for.
> Q: How worried were you that you'd get caught and sent back to prison?
> A: I tried not to think about getting caught as I was doing it. That's something you really just kind of keep on the back burner until it actually happens, and then you start worrying.

And a burglar reported similarly:

> Q: How worried were you when you all did these burglaries that you'd get caught for it?
> A: Well, personally, you try not to think about it while you're doing it because if you start thinking about it really bad before you do it, it's going to make you nervous and more apt to make mistakes. So you try not to worry about it.

Not only did thinking of risks distract the criminal from concentrating on the logistics of the crime, but it was also considered unlucky or negative-results producing. Each of the thirty-eight (63 percent) who used this technique of neutralization stated that he typically attempted to think positively to produce positive results rather than think about the potential negative consequences. By not thinking negatively, they believed they could minimize the chances of negative consequences coming to fruition.

Q: What were you worried about as you thought of doing that burglary?
A: You don't worry about nothing, man. You do that and something bad just might happen, you know. Think positive, you know. Once you start worrying you might bring it to pass.

This neutralization technique influenced their decisions in two related ways. First, the process of blocking out negative thoughts enabled them to avoid assessing risk or having their actions thwarted by risk. Second, their belief in the power of positive thinking and how that influenced their definition of the situation as risky or not, had very real consequences for them in making the decision and completing the act.

Conclusion

This study made use of the analytical concept "neutralization techniques" in relation to this sample of repetitive property offenders. This sample relied on neutralization techniques to facilitate action, in their case both decisions and crimes. All sixty relied on the use of one or more techniques during their decisions to commit crimes. Given the use of such techniques during decision making, criminal decision problems seem to be resolved in a less than rational fashion and not in line with theoretical decision making, especially the economic model of decision making. Although Sykes and Matza (1957) applied these techniques to juvenile delinquency, they are useful analytical concepts for criminal decisions and actions among a sample that is very problematic for society—repetitive property criminals. In Sykes and Matza's study, guilt was neutralized among the delinquents. This study shows that more than guilt must be neutralized for crime to occur. Both fear and anxiety about the upcoming criminal action and its potential consequences must be neutralized in order for the decision to be made to participate in the crime and for the actor to participate in it.

Empirical criminal decision making appears to depart from theoretical decision making on this point. Deterrence theory emphasizes the threat of punishment to induce conformity as a means of social control. Deterrence and decision-making theories also highlight the importance of the actor's assessment of the potential costs and benefits of behavior options. This study indicates that this sample of repetitive property criminals was able to neutralize their perceptions of negative consequences, however serious. Because they used one or more neutralization techniques described here, they did not assess or calculate the potential formal and informal consequences of their actions. Therefore, they were uncontrolled and undeterred.

This type of decision making may not be that different from non-criminal decisions that are made using neutralization techniques. Drinking alcohol and conversing with cohorts are common occurrences during both legitimate and illegitimate decision making. Law-abiding individuals engage in risky decisions (e.g., making purchases of substantial monetary value, traveling internationally, participating in athletic events) and commonly use techniques that help them neutralize their anxieties of possible negative outcomes. This may be the nature of human behavior, regardless of the decisions and actions.

Let's Do It: Deciding to Commit a Crime   6

> We gotta stay cool tonight Eddie
> Cause man we got ourselves out on that line,
> And if we blow this one
> They ain't gonna be looking for just me this time,
> And all we gotta do is hold up our end,
> Here stuff this in your pocket
> It'll look like you're carrying a friend,
> And remember just don't smile,
> Change your shirt, tonight we got style.
>   —Bruce Springsteen, ''Meeting Across the River''

Previous researchers, when addressing the issue of crime specificity in decision-making research, suggest that the mode of resolving criminal decision problems may be related to the type of crime under consideration (e.g., Cornish and Clarke, 1987). Specificity may then be important when seeking individuals' explanations for their choosing to commit a particular crime over no crime at all (i.e., no action), a particular crime over another crime (i.e., displacement), or a particular crime over a legal alternative action. Researchers recently suggested that to differentiate between the resolutions of a variety of criminal decision problems, researchers should obtain a description of a *specific* crime rather than crime generally. This would allow reconstructions of specific events, whereas a discussion of their commission of crime in general would not. For example, to determine the factors that comprise the decision to shoplift, a specific incident of shoplifting would need to be examined. Likewise, to determine the factors that comprise the decision to burgle, a specific incident of burglary would also need to be examined.

Thus, much of each interview with the sixty participants focused on one specific crime, the events leading up to that crime, and most important, the individual's thoughts and conversations during the actual decision to commit the crime. The crime itself and the target they selected were only of peripheral interest. Rather, the respondents were asked to recall the most recent crime they had committed and could remember clearly.[1] At that point in the interview, we then temporally reconstructed as many events as we could that both preceded the crime and that occurred during the crime itself. The emphasis, however, was on the decision to commit the crime. Focused attention was given to those variables of central importance within theoretical decision-making processes, namely, the individual's knowledge and perceptions of the likely positive and negative consequences of his actions.

Perceptions of Formal Punishment

Law-abiding citizens find it unfathomable that individuals have the ability to do something wrong and illegal without considering the risks that could occur. We assume that individual criminals think about the risks they take when choosing to commit a crime. Our public policies are designed to send threatening signals that deviance will not be tolerated and lawbreakers will be punished for their crimes. We create law, we install police forces, we establish courts, and we build increasing numbers of prisons for lawbreakers, and hence find it inconceivable that risk is not considered by such criminals. But, for this sample of criminals who we certainly would like to see deterred from committing crimes, risk represented little threat and, as a result, they went undeterred.

What is it about the nature of their decision making and their perceptions of legal punishment that explains this lack of deterrent effect? Three themes emerged from this study that explain an absence of deterrent effects on their decisions and actions and how they incorporated the threat of punishment into their decision making. First, they believed and hence operated under the assumption that they would not get caught for their crimes. The most active criminals, persistent offenders, knew from personal experience that the probability was low. In fact, recent research shows that the probability of arrest and imprisonment is less than the general public may like to believe. For example, one out of every three crimes is reported; one out of five reported offenses results in arrest; one out of two people arrested are formally charged; nine out of ten people charged are convicted; and one out of every two persons convicted receive prison sentences. Thus, the chances of being arrested are one in fifteen (Wright, 1985) or about as likely as being struck by lightning (Becker, 1970).

Second, they made decisions based on their belief that if they were caught they would be imprisoned for a relatively short period of time. Third, they made decisions to commit crimes based on their belief that prison was a nonthreatening environment. Each of these themes is explicated below and suggests that when the most active property offenders made their habitual decision to commit a crime, they operated beyond the long arm of the law and those policies designed to deter criminal behavior.

Beliefs about Arrest

All sixty respondents in this study reported that they and nearly every thief they had ever known simply did not think about possible legal consequences of their actions. This is especially true for very high-rate criminals who are of grave concern to deterrence-minded policy makers. Rather than thinking of the negative consequences of their actions, those offenders reported thinking primarily of the benefits that they anticipated from their actions.

Deterrence and decision-making theories inform us that risk theoretically is conceptualized and evaluated prior to acting. Again, contrary to decision-making theories, those few participants who conceptualized the possible negative consequences of committing a crime reported that they did not evaluate the consequences. They managed to put those thoughts of negative consequence out of their minds so they would be able to participate in the risky act. Their fear was neutralized as they turned away from signs of danger. Hence, this research suggests that the policy of influencing behavior through punitive policies for repeat property criminals may be ineffective, and has little empirical support.

Even more important, the respondents reported they rarely thought of being captured or being incarcerated in prison. Fifty-two of the sixty reported they simply believed they would not get caught and refused to think beyond that. One twenty-nine-year-old rural burglar and I had the following conversation:

> Q: Come on now. You're not saying you didn't think about getting caught, are you?
> A: I never really thought about getting caught until, pow, you're in jail, you're in juvenile or something. That's when you go to think about it.

And an inner-city hustler reported he had similar thoughts.

> Q: So how much do you think you feared getting caught?
> A: I didn't. I never did think about it really. Not to a point that it would make me undecided or anything like that. I knowed I wasn't supposed to get caught. I just figured every time I wouldn't get caught. I never thought that I would get caught for nothing that I did.

During the crime, thinking of risks was distracting and interfered with performing well in the task they had chosen. I asked a thirty-three-year-old burglar who specialized in stealing kitchen appliances from newly-built apartment complexes about his thoughts of risks prior to committing a crime.

> Q: As you did burglaries, what came first—the crime or thinking about getting caught for the crime?
> A: The crime comes first because it's enough to worry about doing the actual crime itself without worrying about what's going to happen if you get caught.

Even those who knew full well the possible consequences of their actions functioned with the belief that they would not be apprehended or suffer negatively. A twenty-nine-year-old armed robber described how the decision to do a crime was made even though he was aware of potentially negative consequences.

> Q: So, it sounds like as you were approaching an armed robbery you thought about going to prison. And you said you also knew that your mama knew what you were into, and you said that bothered you. And you also just now said you were worried about getting killed or killing somebody. So knowing all those things . . . how did you manage to go ahead and do the armed robbery?
> A: I was doing it just to get money. I didn't really think about all the trouble I'd end up in or anything.

Nearly all claimed to have rarely thought of the potential legal consequences of criminality. The following statement was volunteered by the second oldest sample member—a sixty-year-old armed robber.

> A: I never cared about the risks. I don't think any man can care about the risk or he wouldn't do it. I would never let anything stop me from doing something because of the danger or the risk.

And the following conversation about risk took place with a thirty-three-year-old burglar serving his third prison sentence:

> Q: These burglaries you committed, did you worry much about getting caught while you were doing them?
> A: No.
> Q: What about afterwards?
> A: No-o-o. I didn't give a damn. And the police couldn't catch a damn cold if it wasn't for the snitches.

Like this individual, nearly all claimed to have rarely thought about the potential legal consequences of criminality.

The decision-making process does not appear to have

been one of rational evaluation or calculation between perceived benefits and risks. Rather, the decision was one where the benefits only were considered and risks were (1) rarely thought about or (2) minimally considered but put out of their minds. Risk was a distraction to some individuals, who eventually were able to rid themselves of it. The decision was one of how to do the crime, predicated on the anticipated benefits alone and not the calculated results of the benefits versus the risks. The decision was one of coping with the action by putting the possible negative consequences out of mind—perceptions of consequences that distracted them from the act itself. A few reported that they could not commit a crime if the negative thoughts lingered in their minds. If they were unable to rid themselves of the perceptions of possible negative consequences, they would not go through with the act that they had previously decided to do. (See chapter 7 for an explanation of this dimension of their decision making.) Among this sample, risk was not a variable that appeared in the calculus of typical crimes. When risk surfaced, it was evaluated (e.g., the individual asked if it was empirical or instinctive) and acted upon. It was typically cast aside and considered a hindrance to the task at hand.

Beliefs about Lengthy Prison Sentences

Many of the offenders had unrealistic or erroneous perceptions of the punishment severity for the crime they committed. Each participant reported that they knew their actions were illegal and therefore did their best to avoid capture. But, thirty-two of the participants did not know the severity of the punishment for that particular act until after their arrest. Most learned the "going rate" for certain crimes after their arrest rather than before (Walker, 1985). Their perceptions of the severity of legal sanction were unrealistic. Therefore, risk was weighted less than it ideally should have been. One armed robber, for example, thought that his first armed robbery conviction would result in a probationary sentence rather than a lengthy prison sentence. He never considered his chances of going to prison for a lengthy sentence.

Q: So, before you learned the penalty for armed robbery, did you know that you could go to the penitentiary for it?
A: I hadn't never got caught for robbery or nothing. I thought I'd go to jail and they'd put me on probation or something the first two times. So I really didn't pay too much attention to the penalty because I knew if I got caught that first time I might spend a few days in jail and I knew that my first time . . . I could get probation since it was my first offense. After my first conviction, five years for robbery, I really found out the penalty.

These men typically underestimated the prescriptive punishment for their crimes by believing that prison sentences would be considerably shorter than they actually were. I posed the following question to an inner-city offender who typically committed both armed robbery and strong-armed robbery.

Q: Did you have knowledge of the potential penalty for doing [strong-armed robbery]?
A: In the state of Tennessee, absolutely not. This class X crime penalty that's supposed to be a deterrent . . . I wasn't aware of any class X, I wasn't aware of any penalties whatsoever.[2]

The rationality of their decisions is questionable since they could not have realistically considered the possible outcomes of their actions. They were predisposed to calculate erroneously because they assessed the degree of punishment unrealistically. I asked a participant who specialized in burglary about his worries of incarceration as a juvenile.

Q: Did you know you could get some time as a juvenile for burglary?
A: Everybody told me, said "Hey, all they're going to do is give you probation."

They, therefore, resolved criminal decision problems without full knowledge about the real possible outcomes of various decisions and actions.

Beliefs about the Prison Environment

Prior to their first incarceration, when thinking about being sentenced to prison, these men had typical thoughts about the types of threats in such an environment (e.g., physical and verbal abuse, threats of sexual assault, restricted contact with the outside world). Such thoughts of prison, obviously, were not threatening enough to deter them. During their first incarceration, they concluded that the state's punishment for committing property crimes was not that severe. In other words, the worst punishment that the state could impose on them as property offenders, they discovered, could be endured relatively easily and was viewed from that time on as no great threat. The following dialogue with a twenty-eight-year-old burglar with a tenth grade education illustrates how he came to define prison as a fairly insignificant threat and how he also came to believe it contributed to his manhood.

Q: Prison must not be much of a threat to you.
A: It's not. Prison wasn't what I thought it was.
Q: What do you mean by that?
A: When I went in it . . . at that point in time it was kind of an awful thing to go to prison. That's what I had always heard. But, when I got there and then found out, "Well, hell, look who is here. I didn't know he was here or they was here." And then I seen that I'm a man just like they are and I can make it. And I went and come back so quick.

These individuals also learned the "ins and outs" of the correctional system (e.g., sentence reduction for "good and honor time"). They were then able to rationalize their sentences more easily by knowing that they actually would not serve their full sentence. After learning the ropes of the system, they calculated a second prison sentence as a fairly insignificant threat. Even so, there is no evidence from this study to substantiate the commonly held belief that a longer prison sentence or a harder time in prison would have sent a more threatening signal to these men as they decided to do crime. The conversation below is with a forty-eight-year-old who had committed hundreds of residential burglaries and who was serving his sixth prison sentence.

> Q: When I asked you how much time you did, you said, "Nothing, eighteen months." Did that not seem like much time to you?
> A: I always thought it wasn't nothing because I went and did it and come on back here. But it really wasn't eighteen months, it was thirteen months and something. See they give me eighteen months, see they give me so much off for good behavior. Just like this time I'm doing now. To you fifteen years would be a lot of time because you don't quite understand it. But, after you get into the system here then they give you so many points for this and so many points for that, and when you get through looking at that you really don't have to stay as long as you might think.

Thirty-six of these respondents reported that the possibility of incarceration was no threat to them and, as a result, was not calculated as a serious negative consequence. They typically did not think about formal, legal sanctions when deciding to commit crimes. Even those few who did consider the potential for legal punishment and those who had previously encountered legal punishment did not perceive it as a great threat.[3]

Although risk was relatively unimportant to them in their youth, there is evidence that they worried more about the risk of arrest and incarceration as they grew older. They also believed that, as they aged, their chances of arrest and incarceration increased. From their self-reporting, thoughts of formal punishment were rarely considered, but such thoughts do change with age (see also Shover, 1985). Table 6.1 illustrates the dynamics of their formal risk perceptions across three age periods.

While serving their first prison sentence, these offenders experienced a typical education about prison lifestyles and learned for the first time about prison sentences and the going rate for various crimes (Walker, 1985). For most of them, this

Table 6.1 Self-Reported Worries About Arrest and Incarceration (by Percent and Age Category)

Response	Juvenile[a]	Young Adult[b]	Adult[c]
Never or occasionally worried about arrest	60 %	56.7%	21.7%
Never or occasionally worried about going to jail	66.7	60	28.3
Believed their chances of arrest were low (1-4 on an 8-point scale)[d]	61.7	51.7	21.7
Believed their chances of incarceration were low (1-4 on an 8-point scale)[d]	60	50	18.3

a. Juvenile period refers to younger than age 18
b. Young adult period refers to the ages 18 through 26
c. Adult period refers to age 27 and older
d. Responses are based on an 8-point Likert scale where 1 is representative of their belief that they had no chance of being arrested or incarcerated and 8 representing a certain chance. The respondents were asked to indicate their perceptions of their chances for the three age periods. These figures represent cumulative percentages for numbers 1 through 4 on the 8-point scale (i.e., their beliefs that their chances of arrest and incarceration were low).

represented new knowledge. Afterwards, some offenders desisted from crime for a time. Those who desisted attribute their decision to (1) their new knowledge of legal punishment and the threat it imposed and (2) interpersonal changes in their lives (e.g., newfound family commitments, abstinence from drugs and alcohol, legitimate employment). During this period, some claimed to have considered and pursued legitimate alternatives to crime for the first time since they began committing crimes frequently. Many also reported going through phases of desistance which were not related to the threat of legal sanction. Rather, the phases were related to periods in their lives when conditions were positive and rewarding.

There is some mild support from these findings for temporary deterrence, since a few did desist for a time reportedly because of the threat of legal punishment. Recent research suggests that desistance "is not necessarily permanent and may simply be part of a continuing process of lulls in the offending of persistent criminals" (Clarke and Cornish, 1985:

173). Thus, these respondents are among those who cyclically or temporarily desist from crime (Petersilia et al., 1978; Rowe et al., 1990). From the findings among this sample, the most significant indictment of deterrence theory and deterrence-guided policy is that the majority who temporarily desisted reportedly did so for reasons other than the threat of legal sanction.

Those who did not desist for a time and continued committing crimes after their first incarceration changed their decision making in one of two ways. Some thought about the possibility of legal sanction much more than they ever had before. This often led to, at best, improvements in planning crimes. Others claimed that they continued to simply not think about the legal consequences of their actions, a neutralization technique used among this sample to enable them to decide to commit crimes.

While committing crimes, nearly all sixty respondents (N-51) considered themselves immune from arrest and incarceration, although they believed that every habitual criminal will eventually be arrested. They internalized and exhibited in their profession what Tom Wolfe (1979) referred to among test pilots as "the right stuff." Their belief in their own immunity disallowed adequate consideration of the likelihood of legal consequences.

Still, two participants in particular described being "torn" during their decision making—torn between whether or not to commit the crime. Their indecisiveness was exasperating to them and when describing their decisions to me, they were not all that clear as to why and how they finally chose the particular course of action they did choose. It is not that they were all that committed to their decision to commit a crime but rather they were committed to making some decision. They did consider the risks but they also considered the benefits from the crime. They did not make the decision based on some rational calculation but rather out of their desire to get beyond their indecisiveness. From the following dialogue with a thirty-seven-year-old burglar, we see how he made the decision to commit a crime in a frustrated manner and by "throwing up his hands."

Q: I've heard some of the other fellows I've talked to mention an expression similar to what you used then when you said, "Fuck it, I'll just go ahead and do it." Can you explain that to me? What did it mean to you when you said that to yourself, at that time?

A: When you say, "Fuck it" you don't want to deal with it you just, whatever is up you're going for it. When you say "Fuck it," you're saying "Fuck it, I ain't going to worry about this no more." You ain't going to worry about nothing, you're fixing to go out there and just do whatever it is to do to get it. It's a problem that's up now that you don't want to deal with. So, you're running from the problem.

The second individual who made decisions in this manner was a thirty-eight-year-old armed robber serving his second prison sentence for the armed robbery that he described to me. He, like the burglar just quoted, described struggling with himself and his indecisiveness as he eventually made the decision to commit the crime, all the while waiting for his would-be victims. He described being undecided but then making a frustration-laden decision.

Q: So you stood around for about forty-five minutes waiting on them?
A: Right.
Q: What kinds of things did you think about?
A: I'm thinking, "Must I do this here or must I not?" I said, "I don't need to do this here." And I just said, "I'm going to do it, I'm going to just do it, I'm going to do it."

Although the decisions described here are in relation to crime and criminal decision making, such actions stemming from indecisiveness are not unique to criminal decision problems. Law-abiding individuals daily resolve legitimate noncriminal problems in much the same way. They decide by "throwing up their hands," so to speak, in exasperation. Thus, criminal decisions apparently are made not that differently from non-criminal decisions.

The great majority of these sixty criminals never thought of punishment or capture and did not feel guilty about what they had done. This is not to imply that they are amoral misfits, for my findings and earlier studies suggest that offenders are moral individuals who experience guilt feelings at some point in their criminal careers (e.g., Frazier and Meisenhelder, 1985). Even while frequently engaging in criminal actions, these offenders knew their actions were wrong. But, they were able to rationalize their feelings due to desire or necessity, or they were able to put the wrongfulness of their actions out of their minds and not dwell on them. Likewise, the offenders did not desire punishment.

Perceptions of Informal Punishment

Informal punishments are those beyond the parameters of the legal system. Informal punishment risks typically include sanction or punishment by one's parents, spouse, employer, peers, or significant others. Informal sanctions, however, represent much more far-reaching controls than simply the fear of sanction. They also include thoughts of disappointing significant others, such as family members or employers, the fear of losing a job or having difficulty securing employment in the future. The potential for informal sanctions theoretically acts as a control mechanism and hence serves as a deterrent to deviant behavior and to crime. The effects of these individuals' perceptions of informal sanctions were pursued during the interviews with each of the sixty criminals during their descriptions of a specific crime that they had committed. The findings indicate, not surprisingly, that deterrent effects from the potential for informal sanctions appear to have been nearly nonexistent.

These participants reported that they rarely worried about their family discovering they were committing crimes. The participants were asked if, while deciding to commit a crime, they thought of their parents and the effects on their parents. Almost all reported they did not think of them or worry that they would disappoint them or negatively affect their lives. This is odd since nearly all sixty reported that their parents represented the most significant others in their lives.

They simply did not think about the possible hardships that would be imposed on their family as a result of their arrest or incarceration. When they finally witnessed firsthand the difficulties their family endured, they saw the results of their criminal actions, often for the first time in their lives.[4] One individual offered a sobering example of the effects that his crimes had on his family as he described how he, accompanied by his mother and girlfriend, had to face a shopkeeper to whom he had passed a forged check.

> A: Well, when we got over there, the dude looked at me, and said, "Is this your son?" And she said "Yeah, do you have the picture? Would you let me see the picture?" He showed her the picture and sure enough it was a picture of me standing up there signing the check to get it cashed. So no way out. And my mom looked at me, man, and I seen that hurt in her eyes, and I just didn't know what to say. But then it hurt me just that much more because my girlfriend was standing behind me and she saw it too and it just, it was like I just shattered two lives right there, man. At that very moment I felt remorse. I felt bad about it.

During these conversations about the hardships their families had endured because of these men's crimes, the participants would often volunteer information about prison life as it related to negative effects on their family. One particular prisoner, who had committed burglaries and auto thefts at a high rate after becoming addicted to drugs, indicated once again that it typically was not until after arrest or imprisonment that the criminals considered the negative affects of their criminality on their families.

> Q: What are the worst things about doing time?
> A: Well, one of the worst is like when your family comes to visit you. You see them leave and see a lot of pain and a lot of hurt in their eyes. You know yourself that you're doing alright, but it hurts them a lot worse than it does you. You can see that. It's plain.

The fear of informal sanctions in one form or another from their friends was completely nonexistent. For example, according to reports of these participants, the potential for disappointing their friends who discovered they were committing crimes, or any thoughts about the effects of their incarcerations on these friendships, had no effect whatsoever on them, their criminal activity, or their criminal decision making. Because the friends of most of these individuals were also thieves, their behavior was not viewed by their associates and friends as deviant, but rather as normal, acceptable behavior. The following dialogue illustrates how most of their friends also committed crimes, as one thirty-six-year-old high-rate shoplifter and armed robber ("Floyd," in chapter 8) turned the tables on the researcher and did the questioning. The following questions are his and the answers mine.

Q: Okay, let me ask this here. Didn't the people that you grew up with always do crimes and stuff?
A: There were some people that I knew that were always into crimes, you know, like shoplifting. But as far as people I hung around with into more serious things—
Q: Such as?
A: Burglary or armed robbery . . . breaking and entering.
Q: Would you believe that, I don't have nothing personal against your crowd, but I never remember going to school with them. It seemed like everybody that I knew was damn near into the same things that I was, or they was wanting to be, or claiming to be, or something.
A: That's surprising.
Q: Well, your story is also surprising.

Thus, informal sanction risks were almost nonexistent in these men's lives and as a result, their perceptions of informal sanctions were calculated as insignificant. Their decision making about crime typically did not take into account the possibility of informal sanctions or the likelihood of negatively affecting their life or anyone else's. It was not until after they had been arrested, jailed, or imprisoned that they appreciated the gravity of their actions and the effects on family members and interpersonal relationships.

Conclusion

This chapter provides data on the way that decisions to commit crimes were made by this sample of repeat offenders. Nearly all sixty reported they rarely considered the threat of capture, arrest, and imprisonment and that risk was considered a nuisance rather than a real, tangible threat. Risk-related thoughts were considered distracting from their prime objective—committing the crime. Thus, many were simply able to not think about risks and to put them out of their minds.

These findings are incongruous with rational decision-making theories. Decisions, theoretically, are made by calculating the potential benefits and risks. Among this sample, such calculations remain theoretical, for there is little empirical support here for calculated action. Even risky legitimate decisions seemingly are calculated with more care and finesse than decisions found among these men.

For the behavior of this sample of very active repeat offenders, deterrence theory and policy lack an adequate explanation. This sample represents a criminal population that has committed a disproportionate number of street crimes and has done so with little concern for the law, arrest, or imprisonment. A crime control policy that uses harsher penalties may deter those individuals who either do not commit crimes or commit crimes infrequently, but appears dubiously successful when applied to those individuals who frequently commit crimes. Although these offenders represent a population that we as a society would most like to deter from committing property crimes, they view themselves as immune from criminal sanction and hence go undeterred. They tend to believe that they simply will not be apprehended for their criminal actions and if they are, they will be imprisoned for a very short time. Those who actually consider the possibilities of imprisonment view prison as a non-threatening environment and believe their stay will be short.

Although much has been written on the risk-benefit calculus, it is somewhat misleading for understanding criminal decision making. The decision-making process among this sample of chronic offenders appears to not be one of rational evaluation or calculation between potential benefits and risks. Rather, the decision was one where only the benefits were considered and risks were (1) rarely thought about or (2) minimally considered but were put out of mind.

NOTES

1. The individuals had earlier been asked to disclose the numbers and types of crimes they had committed, including both crimes for which they had been arrested and crimes that escaped official detection, that is, crimes that they had committed that they had not been arrested or punished for (see table 2.3 for the number and types of self-reported crimes). But for a description of their decision making, I had each focus on only one typical crime that he had committed.

2. Class X legislation was passed in the state of Tennessee in the early 1980s. As a component of "sentencing reform," it mandates that individuals convicted of committing certain crimes (e.g., armed robbery and burglary) be sentenced to a determinant, fixed period of "flat time" in prison.

3. I provide descriptive statistics on two components of their decision making that demand further explanation. True, thirty-two of the sixty did not know the punishment severity for the crime they committed and thirty-six did not find imprisonment a threat. However, twenty-eight did know the punishment severity and twenty-four did find prison threatening. These latter individuals managed to make the decision to commit crimes anyway. They managed to do so with the aid of neutralization techniques. They used these techniques to complete the risky action and then thought about the risk they had run afterwards. For example, forty-one of the sixty typically relied on alcohol or drugs to deaden their thoughts of negative consequences; sixteen of the sixty relied on the calming effect of conversation with their cohorts prior to committing a typical crime; fifty-four of the sixty (at some point in their lives) relied on the expertise of their older and hence wiser cohorts; and thirty-eight of the sixty managed to block

out negative thoughts of capture and imprisonment until after the crime. These neutralization techniques (explicated in chapter 5) represent tactics that allowed these individuals to avoid the fear of formal punishment.

    4. Many now claim they do not want to cause their family similar hardships in the future. Those thirty-three participants who reported during the second interview that they had successfully desisted, claimed that if they considered committing a crime, they would consider the effects of their criminal actions on their parents.

7
Whoa Now: Deciding Not to Commit a Crime

Doubtless, these men represent undeterred criminals who have not only committed crimes at a disproportionately high rate, but also flauntingly committed crimes with nearly total disregard for the sociojudicial system, the threat of being sanctioned by that system, and the potential for subsequent interpersonal problems. They communicated their disregard for sanction threats as they described their mode of making decisions about committing crimes (as described in chapters 6 and 8). Although every effort was made to assess the internal validity of the data and to communicate to them that I was "con-wise," they did occasionally slip into bragging about their exploits. This is not unusual. It has been observed by both popular and scientific studies that criminals have enormous egos, that is, they enjoy weaving outlandish tales of their outlaw behavior and their incredible success at avoiding capture and punishment.[1] When I engaged these participants in conversations about their crimes, they often described their exploits with such passion that it was as if they had been transported to that wild, free, and adventurous time of their lives—a time markedly different from the drab, boring, and confining environment of prison.

To understand these descriptions of their criminal exploits and especially the decisions they made about crime was the most important objective of this study. After all, these men represent those who have gone undeterred over a period of years of criminal activity—despite the possibility of a host of potential punishments. But, from those several hours of conversing with them (and based on simple common sense) it became just as clear that they certainly did not commit a crime every time they planned on doing so. What of those times when they had planned on committing a crime, those times when they had decided to, and then decided not to? Could it be that police visibility, sophisticated burglar alarms, bright lights, and other forms of target hardening produced deterrence? Or could other variables have accounted for those times? These questions emerged during the formative stages of this research and were pursued with each of the sixty sample members. I thought from the onset of this research that those occasions when they decided not to commit a crime might tell us something about situations that produce a deterrent effect, even among repeat offenders who have gone mostly undeterred. To understand if those situations and decisions do occur and what may account for them, I had each of the respondents focus on another time when they were contemplating a crime.

During the interviews, each interviewee was asked to describe the most recent time that they could remember clearly when they made a conscious decision not to commit a crime. When I asked this question during the early stages of the interviews, every participant related a specific time when he made such a decision. They reported that their criminal intentions were displaced for one of two reasons: a police officer had been seen in the vicinity, or a person who could witness the crime was observed in the area. During the early stages of conducting interviews, I asked a question much like the following:

Q: Was there a time when you were thinking of committing a crime and then decided not to?

Each time I asked that question I received an answer much like the following:

> A: Yeah. Well, a couple of times it happened that we rode out to where we had seen a good-looking house the day before and we passed the police. Just like they knew we was going to be out there. And we decided to just not do it.

Or an answer such as this:

> A: Yeah. We had a place lined up and the goddamn nosy neighbors got to looking at us, real suspicious like. So we didn't do it.

When this consistent pattern among their responses emerged, the question was then qualified in such a way as to limit their reconstructions to specific times when they were displaced for reasons other than when they saw the police or a would-be witness.[2] It is not very interesting to know that they chose not to commit a crime because of police or witness presence. This deterrent or preventive effect is practically a given and represents a decision that if not made could be interpreted as beyond the realm of rational thought. Rather, I was looking for a decision that they made based on some calculation—a calculation that led them to believe that risks were too great or rewards were too few—and not for those times when we would expect them to not commit a crime. I rephrased the question in such a way that they were limited in their selection of particular incidents in which they chose not to commit a crime. The newly formed question was typically:

> Q: Other than when you saw the police or a neighbor or witness, was there a time when you decided not to commit a crime you had been thinking of doing?

When the participant then recalled the most recent incident, the interview focused on the same topics of inquiry as those during the conversation about the decision to commit a crime. A concentrated effort was made to reconstruct events and conversations preceding and during the decision itself. Their retrospective accounts of conversations with others and their thoughts were probed to understand the way the decision problem was framed and to inform us of how the decision to not commit a specific crime was arrived at.

As I asked this newly formulated question of the participants, few could recall such a time when they decided not to commit a crime for reasons other than when they saw the police or a potential witness. Deciding not to commit a crime due to target-hardening devices (e.g., burglar alarms, closed circuit TV systems, automobile alarms, etc.) was hardly ever mentioned by these men. When such an obstacle to crime commission was mentioned, they typically reported that they either disengaged the alarm or found another target without such devices. Of those who could recall a specific time when they decided not to commit a crime, all described a time when things did not "feel right." The following conversation with a twenty-eight-year-old burglar illustrates this concept of "things not feeling right," or what he referred to as "inner feelings."

> Q: Did you ever have a chance to commit a crime such as one of these burglaries or robberies and then decide not to for some reason?
> A: Yeah. I know of one incident. It was just my inner feelings told me that something wasn't right.

They all described times when their intuition led them to believe that some kind of risk was imminent, although they may not have visually seen anything about the particular crime or target they were getting ready for. They emphatically related to me that their decisions were not because they saw something that did not look right. Rather they felt that something was not right. They described this inner feeling with a variety of labels, but each, I discovered, referred to the same phenomenon. For example, they described the feeling as "butterflies," a "gut feeling," and an "instinct." A twenty-nine-year-old, very high-rate business burglar and I had the following conversation about this topic.

> Q: Other than seeing the police, did you ever decide not to commit a burglary for some reason?
> A: Sure. If I had bad feelings about it I wouldn't do it. You just have to go on your feelings, you know, when you're doing something like that because you've got no other way of knowing what's happening.
> Q: Is that like a gut-level feeling?
> A: It was a sick feeling like disaster was in front of you.

And a thirty-two-year-old high-rate armed robber reported the following after I asked him for the same type of information.

> A: I've had places planned to rob and got a bad feeling about it and not done it. That robbery would be on my mind and I just took it as something telling me, "That ain't going to work. Don't do it." So, I didn't do it. I never went against my feelings.

Among those participants who admitted that the potential for arrest and imprisonment prevented them from committing an occasional crime, I was especially curious about how this instinctual feeling fit into their criminal calculus. I had the following conversation about how intuition might account for the decision not to commit a crime with an inner-city hustler (Archie in chapter 8), who informed me that he occasionally thought about the possibility of punishment.

> Q: Of the times that you didn't go through with a crime, what percentage of those times were because you thought you could go to prison?
> A: Twenty to 25 percent.
> Q: What percentage was because of this intuition feeling you're talking about?
> A: Seventy-five percent.

This individual's responses are representative of this sample of offenders. The overwhelming majority claimed that when they were deterred for reasons other than police presence, they typically were deterred (i.e., chose not to commit the crime) because they were following their instincts. This is important for deterrence policy, for again, evidence suggests that not only is deterrence an ineffectual policy for repetitive offenders, but also that other reasons—reasons that cannot be clearly articulated and co-opted by state law—account for decisions to not commit crimes. Such internal or instinctual reasons may be beyond the scope of rational decision-making theories and also may be indicative of decision making among both criminals and non-criminals.

A few insightful individuals were able to relate their experiences of deciding not to commit a crime to similar intuitive feelings about risky legitimate experiences. After a high-rate auto parts thief explained to me that he had decided not to commit a crime due to instinctual feelings, I attempted to have him relate his feelings to something other than crime. His criminal specialty at that time was stealing and then selling expensive Corvette tops.

> Q: Can you relate that feeling to any gut-level feeling you've had about other things in your life, besides criminal things?
> A: Well, it'd be like, if you was going to buy a car and you didn't feel like the guy was shooting straight with you. You just had a feeling, "I don't feel like he's telling me the truth." Or, "I feel like if I buy this car and get down the road the motor is going to fall out of it." It'd be about the same deal. I feel like, if I get these [Corvette] tops, there's going to be more involved in it than what I anticipate. You know?

And another individual, a high-rate burglar, voluntarily related his instinctual feelings that led to his decision not to commit a crime to a decision unrelated to crime—a decision to not participate in a legal, recreational endeavor.

Q: Had you backed out of crimes before because they just didn't feel right?
A: Yeah.
Q: I've heard some people call the feeling intuition. Is that kind of like intuition?
A: I'm not sure what you'd call that; it's just like you going down here to this river and finding a place to jump in but changing your mind and going to another place to jump in. It's just something that didn't strike you right about that one place so you backed out of it. I don't know what causes it.

Some of the participants were able to decide to do a crime and then commit it even with the feelings of nervousness common among these respondents. The following dialogue illustrates how a twenty-seven-year-old armed robber (Floyd in chapter 8) decided to do the crime even while experiencing these intuitive feelings. He is unusual in this, for the vast majority who alluded to instinctual feelings claimed that they always followed their feelings and chose not to do the particular crime. This particular robber also related this decision to a legitimate decision and act. It is clear that he approached crime as a profession and considered nervousness as one of the hazards of his profession.

Q: Some people have told me about some gut-level feeling— what they called instinct or a sixth sense. They just sense something isn't right.
A: Well, I always get that. You're going to get that before every armed robbery and I'll tell you why. Because you was brought up not to do them. It's the same damn way, man, if you're out on the street and you get you a prostitute and you're taking her to this motel. You've got the same feeling.
Q: Have you ever decided not to go through with a robbery because of that feeling [instinct]?
A: Not that I recall. I know that I'm doing wrong and I'm taking a chance and I just go on with a positive attitude. It's the same way that you got in your car and you started

down here. Right? Okay. What would have happened if you started thinking, "Well, look here, I could have a car wreck around this next corner here?" Are you going to just turn around and go back? It's your job to get here and do that, right? It's the same thing. It's a job to me, so I do my best at it.
Q: What does it feel like, is it a gut-level feeling?
A: It's a scared feeling, it's a do wrong feeling. It's a small feeling of being in school and I've done wrong and here I am sitting in the principal's office, you know? It's a scary feeling. I do get them, yeah, sure. I think everybody does.
Q: When does the feeling leave you?
A: Right after I've got the money.

The majority of the respondents, unlike this robber, considered themselves intuitive and took great pride in following the lead of their intuition. When confronted with intuitive nervousness or "butterflies," they nearly always decided not to commit the crime. They could not point to a concrete factor that led to their decision to not commit the crime. In fact, during the reconstruction of their daily events, conversations, and thoughts leading to the decision to not commit the crime, other than these instinctual feelings (and spotting a cop or witness), no differences were discernible between those occasions when the decision was made to commit a crime and those when the decision was made to not commit a crime.

Conclusion

This chapter describes those times when these repetitive criminals decided to not commit a specific crime, even if it was a type of crime that they had committed previously and that they felt comfortable with. Doubtless, criminals do not commit crimes in the presence of the police or normally in the presence of a witness. These participants confirmed this common sense assumption about criminals and their crimes. Other than those two specific deterrent-producing situations, these participants related that they were deterred from committing crimes because of only one factor—instinct. They followed the lead of their inner feelings and claimed that they were better off for doing so. Although the majority reported that they did not commit crimes when they had those nervous feelings, a very few reported that nervousness is simply part of the criminal act and a component that must be suppressed. Otherwise, according to those few, they would never have committed a crime, since the feelings surfaced prior to every crime.

These findings represent yet another fundamental critique of deterrence-guided public policy. As we learned in previous chapters, some did not know the penalty for their crimes, and those who did know considered the penalty an insignificant threat. And from this chapter we learn that those who, in effect, were deterred and decided not to commit specific crimes, made those decisions because of intangible factors—instinct, butterflies, nervousness—rather than tangible formal or informal sanction threats. Furthermore, those who went undeterred but who also experienced those inner feelings, managed to lay aside those feelings by considering them part of the occupational hazards of a criminal lifestyle and by using neutralization techniques. So, not only does deterrence policy seem inappropriate for this sample, but internal controls also were not effective among those who committed crimes, even if the criminals experienced those inner-control sensations.

A Look Ahead

From the outset, one objective of this research had been to construct types of decision making from among this sample. As the previously discussed components of decision making were used in the interviews, patterns emerged in the form of different types of offenders and decision makers. In the next chapter, these broader components of decision making are related to specific decision-making types that were constructed during this research. These components are made clearer when discussed in relation to specific crime types and modes of decision making. Following each type of decision making, I provide a brief case study that illustrates further the similarities and differences between various types of decision makers in this sample.

NOTES

1. There is a host of published works that well illustrate the criminal ego. Works that tend to make folk heroes out of outlaws are popular readings. Much has been written aggrandizing such outlaws as Frank and Jesse James, John Dillinger, Bonnie and Clyde, Pretty Boy Floyd, Charles Manson, and Ted Bundy. Although we as a society often consider them a scourge, we nonetheless do occasionally place them in positions of folk heroes (Givan, 1988; Tunnell, 1990a).

2. The presence of a witness was often of little importance to the armed robbers in this sample (since victims are also witnesses). They typically sought out targets where there were no witnesses (other than the victim), but on those occasions when there were witnesses at the scene or when witnesses entered the scene during the robbery, the robbers continued the task that they had begun and dealt with the witnesses in a number of ways (e.g., contained them and their activities, robbed them, or ordered them to leave the scene).

A Taxonomy of Criminal Decision Making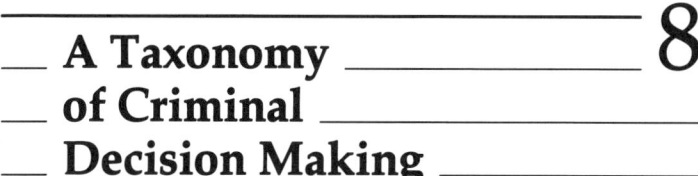

Criminal offender taxonomies have been constructed throughout the history of research on individual criminals. Criminological research on criminals who commit crimes repeatedly has produced such offender types as "chronic," "career" (Blumstein, 1982), "occasional," "habitual," "casual" (Lombroso, 1911; Morris, 1951; Roebuck, 1967), "chronic recidivist" (Walker, 1985), "hard-core," "successful," "unsuccessful" (Shover, 1985), and "intensive" and "intermittent" (Petersilia et al., 1978). These categories have proven useful both in illustrating similarities and dissimilarities among types of criminals and in shaping this particular study of repetitive offenders. In inductive research such as this, when individual criminals' explanations for crime and their decision-making processes are assessed, clearly developed offender types are crucial for better understanding the similarities and dissimilarities between individuals' decisions to commit crime.[1]

A more recent method of constructing offender types uses the individual criminal's frequency of crime commission over a given period of time. Such a frequency of crime commission has been given the label "lambda."[2] Lambda has been defined as "the number of crimes an active offender commits in a unit of time" (Blumstein et al., 1988b: 58). Some researchers, when computing lambda, use as the unit of time the year prior to an individual's incarceration (Chaiken and Chaiken, 1982) and some compute lambda based on "the number of crimes committed divided by the number of years of street time" (Visher, 1986; 172). This frequency of offending represents an individual's rate of crime commission, which distinguishes it from aggregate data found in earlier deterrence-related research (for a fuller explanation see Blumstein et al., 1988a).

While this research was in progress and as the interview data were being analyzed, it became clear that some sample members committed far more crimes than others. And those who committed the greatest number did so at a higher frequency rate than others.

During the data analysis, a question, inspired by recent debates among researchers, emerged. Specifically, are there discernible distinctions in the perceptions of sanction threats (whether formal or informal) and criminal decision making among very active and less active property offenders? To address this question, the interview data were analyzed continuously to make sense of sanction threat perceptions and situational factors among those who reported committing large numbers of crimes and those who reported committing fewer numbers of crime. Self-report data and official case records were used to compile the total number of crimes that each individual committed, his contacts with the criminal justice system, and his mode of resolving criminal decision problems. From these data and the in-depth long interviews with each of the sixty, offender decision-making typologies were constructed.

The following section provides a description of both the subtle and not-so-subtle differences in criminal decision-making types among this sample. Such types are based on both the total number of crimes an individual criminal committed and the way that he incorporated sanction threats (whether real or perceived) into his decision-making processes.

Differentiating Offender Decision-Making Types

Previous researchers who have studied repetitive offenders have constructed operational definitions of lambda as a way of assessing the seriousness of and commitment to criminal careers. For example, Chaiken and Chaiken (1982) defined a high lambda offender as one who had committed eleven or more crimes during a specific time in their lives on the "street." Although helpful, this mode of labeling a high-rate or serious offender seemingly is too narrow in its focus and does not take into account the lulls or periods of desistance in a criminal career. It seems perfectly reasonable to assume that some fairly active criminals could both easily and quickly commit eleven street crimes prior to their incarceration without giving much though to committing themselves to crime as a way of life or to crime as a career. From both this study and recent data from the National Institute of Justice, we learn that those criminals who commit disproportionate numbers of crimes and who represent concerns for society commit far more crimes than we may have thought and some at a daily or near-daily frequency.

To differentiate between high- and low-rate offenders (i.e. very active and less active) among this sample of repetitive criminals, I used a demarcation considerably higher than other researchers have previously used (e.g., Chaiken and Chaiken, 1982; Visher, 1986).[3] Among this sample of offenders, I determined that those who had committed one hundred or more felony crimes during their years of street time did so frequently, and are typed persistent offenders in this study. Those who committed fewer than one hundred did so infrequently and are typed sporadic offenders in this study.[4]

From this sample of repeat offenders, it is clear that persistent offenders have been more successful criminals than sporadic, if by nothing more than the sheer number of crimes they have committed and have avoided punishment for. The persistent offenders have been arrested and punished for a smaller proportion of crimes they committed than the sporadic offenders. Persistents' successes are determined, in part, by their perceptions of sanction threats, their decision making, their commitment to crime as a way of life, and their individual characteristics.

Although there clearly are similarities among previous types and those constructed here, those presented in this work represent offender types based on offenders' responses to a host of open-ended questions about their decisions to commit specific crimes, their self-reported frequency and duration of crime commission, and most important, their reconstructions of their decisions to commit a specific crime.

Further Differentiating Persistent and Sporadic Types

The persistent offender is one who has been criminally active over a long period of time, sees himself as somewhat of a professional, and concentrates on planning more than the sporadic offender. The sporadic criminal offender identified in this research is one who has committed crimes infrequently and often opportunistically. This type is uncommitted to a criminal lifestyle and has a lower "success" record (i.e., they have been punished for a greater percentage of their crimes than the persistent offender). Table 8.1 details the number of

Table 8.1   Total Numbers of Self-Reported Crimes (by Crime and Offender Type)

Crime Type	Persistent	Sporadic
Armed Robbery	935	145
Strong Armed Robbery	887	20
Home Burglary	4,894	117
Business Burglary	2,367	74
Auto Theft	3,327	73
Shoplifting	3,926	114
Buying and Selling Stolen Goods	13,853	103
Forgery	6,401	40
Grand Theft	7,528	53
Petty Theft	3,772	107
Total	47,890	846
Total crimes committeed (persistent & sporadic) = 48,736		

N = 60

Table 8.2 Differentiating Characteristics of Offender Types (by Offender Type and Percent)

	Persistent	Sporadic
Crimes planned alone	44%	11.5%
Alcohol use	23	38.4
Drug addiction	44	7.7

Totals may not equal 100 due to rounding.

self-reported crimes by decision-making types. From these numbers, we see that persistents reported committing far more crimes than sporadics.

Unlike some earlier studies, I did find an association between the number of crimes committed and the offender's decision-making processes. For example, thirty-four of the sixty sample members (56.6 percent) were identified as persistent offenders. Twenty-six individuals (43.4 percent) of the sample were identified as sporadic offenders. Forty-four percent of the persistent offenders had a severe drug addiction—an addiction that demanded daily attention, compared to only 7.7 percent of sporadic offenders (see table 8.2). The drug-dependent individuals were not only dependent on their physically addictive drug but also on easily accessible cash to purchase drugs. Of the thirty-four persistent offenders, only one was employed legitimately and the other thirty-three had defined their situation as one without legitimate alternatives for money. They functioned with the knowledge and mind-set that they had to steal to meet their needs, whether legitimate or illegitimate.

Whenever persistent offenders faced the decision to commit or not commit a crime, it was less of a "decision problem" or dilemma than it was for sporadic offenders. Persistent offenders daily functioned with the predisposition to commit crimes—the decision was not one that required a great deal of pondering. It was a given for them that they would commit crimes to meet their needs. Most did not have or seek any other alternatives to crime. Table 8.3 illustrates those alternatives considered by offender type.

The decisions that they defined as requiring careful

Table 8.3 Alternatives Considered (by Offender Type and Percent)

	Persistent	Sporadic
No alternatives	74%	69%
Another crime	12	0
Borrowing money	1	8
Legitimate work	0	15
Rejection of work ethic	12	8

Totals may not equal 100 due to rounding.

thought and pondering were merely logistical (e.g., planning, target selection, and casing). They knew that theft offered "quick, easy money" unlike a legitimate "square-john" job. They also knew that in their drug-addicted condition, they would not be able to obtain and maintain legitimate employment. Thus, the decision to commit a crime for the persistent offenders was not a decision of "should I" or "shouldn't I" or one of calculation, as the following quote illustrates:

> A: With drugs you don't rationalize. It's just a decision you make. You don't weigh the consequences, the pros, the cons. You just do it.

Although drug addiction was prevalent among persistent offenders, sporadic offenders were those who relied on alcohol. Thirty-eight percent of the sporadic offenders had alcohol problems and used alcohol during decisions to commit crimes compared to 23 percent of persistent offenders (see table 8.2).

Sporadic offenders typically needed some type of encouragement to complete the risky decision—encouragement that came from others or from alcohol. They first decided that they wanted to engage in some type of criminal act and then began drinking to gain enough encouragement to make more specific decisions about the crime and to participate in it. In retrospect, they often blamed their criminal actions on the alcohol rather than on the decision they had made prior to consuming the alcohol. Table 8.2 illustrates that alcohol was used among

Table 8.4 Neutralization Techniques Used (by Offender Type and Percent)

	Persistent	Sporadic
Alcohol and drugs	82%	53%
Conversation with others	8	46
Influence of older person	76	100
Putting risks out of mind	66	50

Totals may not equal 100 due to rounding.

this sample much more frequently by sporadic offenders than persistent, as the following quotes from three sporadic offenders show.

> A: Drinking was the whole problem. That drinking will pump you right up.
> A: That alcohol partly made me just go ahead and do it.
> A: I believe if I never started drinking wine I'd never done it.

Both illegal drugs and alcohol use are shown once again to be important variables within decisions to commit crimes. As tables 8.2 and 8.4 show, drug addiction was an ongoing condition for persistent criminals, and alcohol addiction and consumption were found primarily among sporadic criminals.

Regarding the question of planning their crimes, 44 percent of the persistent offenders planned their crimes compared to 11.5 percent of sporadic offenders (see table 8.2). Also, 47 percent of persistent offenders committed their crimes alone compared to 30.7 percent of sporadic offenders. The persistent offenders approached their planned actions with greater knowledge about the decision problem and with better logistical information for solving that problem. They were also prepared to act criminally nearly every day. Those sporadic offenders who typically committed crimes with others often relied on psychological encouragement to complete the act. Although the sporadic offenders relied on encouragement, the encouragement was minimal. Previous successful crimes were recalled with pride to illustrate that they had succeeded and could succeed in the crime facing them.

Persistent offenders, unlike sporadics, were those who deliberated, calculated, and planned their crimes and considered crime a career. They approached crime more professionally and viewed it as more than a short-term venture. The persistent offenders considered crime an occupation to the point that they talked about going to work or making some money in reference to their illegal activities.

> Q: What kinds of things did you suggest to him?
> A: I just wanted somewhere where we could go rob something.
> Q: So you suggested you all go somewhere and rob?
> A: Yeah, make some, well, we call it making money.
> Q: So whenever you all said "making money" that's what it meant?
> A: Right.

Sporadic offenders, on the other hand, decided to commit crimes more opportunistically and spontaneously than persistent offenders.

> Q: Tell me about that conversation you all had.
> A: I said, "I know a place I think we can get some money." I asked him if he wanted to do it . . . I knowed the answer was going to be, "Yeah." It wasn't no big discussion. We just did it.

Thus, a significant difference between these types is reflected in their commitment to crime as a way of life, their finesse in planning specific crimes, and their strategies of executing their criminal intentions.

In the remainder of this chapter, these two decision-making types are described further. The persistent offender type is differentiated into three subtypes—the non–drug-addicted, the drug-addicted, and the hustler. A case study of each type is offered as a means of illustrating the differences in criminal decision-making types. The individuals chosen for these case studies were selected for two important reasons.

First, each is representative of his type and second, each was selected because of his insightfulness, reflectivity, and apparent honesty and candor. Those chosen were able to reconstruct and articulate a specific crime that they committed and the events, conversations, thoughts, and decision making that occurred prior to that crime. Such information is essential for understanding the resolution of a specific criminal decision problem.

The following case study of one persistent offender well represents the persistent offenders among this sample. His biography is typical of most non–drug-addicted persistent offenders who are not hustlers. Case studies and further descriptions of the other persistent subtypes and of the sporadic offender follow this case study.

Floyd: A Persistent Offender

Floyd,[5] a product of a broken home, was raised by his mother and stepfather. He lived with them and several siblings in the inner city of a rather large urban area. He characterized his family's socioeconomic class at the time he grew up as lower-working class. He began disliking school at an early age and dropped out after completing only the seventh grade. While reflecting on and describing his educational experiences, it became quite obvious that he seriously disliked school.

Q: You say you hated school? Why did you?
A: I think it was authority more or less. In fact, to this day, I've got a worse hate for school than I do the penitentiary system.

This apparent disgust with authority and authority figures recurred time and time again during much of his self-reporting of his criminal activity and his descriptions of making decisions about various crimes. This repulsion for authority was evident in both his descriptions of committing crimes while in the presence of authority figures and his attitudes about the victims of his crimes. For Floyd victims were often authority figures.

Floyd's earliest criminal involvement was in shoplifting, which also became the first crime that he specialized in.

Q: So was shoplifting the crime you started with?
A: That was my main specialty.

Floyd, like the majority of persistent offenders, nearly always concentrated or specialized in one crime for a period of time and then "graduated" to another specialty area. His career and the careers of other persistent offenders consisted of progressive steps, with each step representing a different crime type or specialty. Most of Floyd's energies, channeled at first into shoplifting, were later redirected into armed robbery. This temporal specialty phenomenon supports the idea of specialization among those who consider crime a profession or a way of life yet drastically differs from the generalist argument that property criminals are uncommitted to any one type of crime and commit crimes opportunistically (e.g., Petersilia et al., 1978; Kempf, 1987). A discussion of the specialist/generalist debate appears in chapter 9.

Floyd claimed that as a juvenile (when he first began committing crimes), he committed between five hundred and six hundred shopliftings. As I attempted to arrive at an estimate of the frequency of his crime commission during this period of his life, I discovered that he was nearly always ready to commit a crime.

A: So how often did you commit them?
A: Anytime I could. Anytime that I only stood a 50 percent chance of making it. Sometimes if I only stood a 25 percent chance of doing it, I would do it, because I enjoyed it. I'm the type of person, man, if I could steal something from way in the back row or if the store manager is standing here and I could take something right under his nose, that's what I'd get.
Q: Why would you prefer that?
A: Because it's more of an accomplishment.

His words not only indicate the frequency with which he shoplifted but also are suggestive of his disdain for authority figures. He thought that by shoplifting "right under his nose" he could pull one over on the manager, make him look foolish, and in effect call into question his authority. The manager represented an authority figure to Floyd and matching wits with him, so to speak, represented a challenge. By outsmarting this authority figure, Floyd surmised he had not only successfully shoplifted but also had acquired something more than the monetary reward from his exploits; he had obtained an intangible nonpecuniary benefit from his act. He reportedly soon developed a taste for shoplifting and the pecuniary and nonpecuniary rewards it offered.

Q: What were your motivations to shoplift then?
A: Because it's easy money [and] it's exciting. But wanting to do it man, wanting to do it. Love to do it. "Love" to do it would be the word.

Floyd committed crimes at a very high rate and was nearly always motivated by the benefits of easy money and excitement. Floyd, however, emphasized the lure and pleasure of excitement more than most persistent offenders, for most reported that committing crime provided only a latent benefit of excitement. Excitement, a psychological expressive benefit, clearly was not a major motivating factor in their decision making. Floyd's assessment represents a departure from other persistent offenders.

He nearly always committed these early crimes with someone else and with almost no planning or conversation about the decision to shoplift. He and his accomplice would simply frequent different stores together with full intentions of stealing whatever and whenever they could. Shoplifting was an adventure that they both found enjoyable and financially rewarding.

Persistent offenders more often than not reported using drugs and alcohol during both their decisions and their crimes. They used them due to their addiction and as neutralization techniques. Although Floyd (and this subtype of persistent offenders) was not addicted to drugs, he nonetheless used them as a way of neutralizing any worries that he might have had. But, his words indicate that he had full intentions of doing crime with or without the use of alcohol or drugs.

> Q: Were you using alcohol or drugs during the period you shoplifted?
> A: Yeah.
> Q: Did you ever use them to build your courage up to shoplift?
> A: No, no. In fact, I could not even blame my shoplifting or whatever I done wrong on drugs or alcohol. I'm sure to a certain extent it did pump you up some, but I would definitely done what I was doing if I didn't have it.

As mentioned in previous chapters, the individual's knowledge of alternative actions, the alternatives available, and alternative decisions they considered are important in describing and analyzing decision making. During the interviews, each of the sixty respondents was asked about such alternatives to the crime and how they arrived at the course of action they decided to pursue. When asked about alternatives that he considered while deciding to commit a crime, Floyd responded typically for persistent offenders.

> Q: Did you see any alternatives at all?
> A: Never looked for none because there wasn't anything that I enjoyed more than shoplifting.

These comments indicate several important points about the way persistent criminals decide to commit crime. First, Floyd represents a criminal who is committed to crime as a way of life and an occupation. Thus, he, like professionals in legitimate occupations, considered no alternatives to the profession that he knew best. Second, having dropped out of school during the seventh grade and having no marketable job skills, Floyd's alternatives were few in number. He was somewhat aware of his limitations for earning a legitimate living. Floyd's response that he did not consider any alternative action to the crime is congruous with reports from other persistent offenders. In fact, of the persistent offenders, 74 percent reported they considered no alternative action to the crime they were considering. Only 12 percent of the persistent offenders reported considering another crime and a mere 1 percent reported a legal alternative—borrowing money (see table 8.3).

When questioned about the potential legal and informal risks that he may have considered, Floyd admitted that he certainly had been aware of some. He, like the majority of the sample, had only a minimal understanding of the penalty for the crime he was committing. He knew enough about the risks to do what he believed was necessary to avoid capture and he believed that he could continue to avoid it. He fully believed that he was skillful and clever enough to avoid arrest and whatever might come afterwards. The only worry he had was during his juvenile years, when he considered the possibility of informal punishment that his mother and stepfather might impose on him. His perceptions of risk, at that time in his career, again are typical of persistent offenders.

Q: Did you know the penalty for shoplifting at that time?
A: I knew one thing. If you got caught you got in trouble, period. As far as ever thinking about being locked up, no, I never really thought about that. If I was to worry about anything it would be my parents catching me.
Q: That was your biggest worry?
A: It was my only worry then.

Floyd soon abandoned his career in shoplifting and delved into burglary for a short period of time before reaching the age of eighteen. Although he was never committed to burglary as a specialty, he claims to have committed between twenty and thirty of them. Rather than taking the initiative in burglary, as he had done with shoplifting and later with armed robbery, Floyd was led into most burglaries by friends and associates.

A: I was always with someone else. Usually because they wanted to do it. I never was much into burglaries. I have never had a desire for burglaries.

Floyd clearly was a leader in both shoplifting and armed robbery. But, being uncommitted to burglary as a specialty, he never exercised his leadership abilities as he had done with shoplifting and later would do with armed robbery.

> Q: Think of things that might have influenced you to commit burglaries.
> A: All the other people, man. I did a burglary because the person next to me or persons next to me wanted to go in that house and do a burglary. So what am I going to do, sit down here until they come back? So, to hell with it, "Let's do a burglary."

It soon became apparent that his desire to be accepted by these significant others who were committed to burglary clearly propelled Floyd into committing a type of crime that he had little interest in. Perhaps since another person or persons suggested the crime and the target, those individuals allowed little opportunity for Floyd to exert his leadership ability. He also reported that he disliked burglary because he believed there were too many uncontrollable variables involved in this type of crime. For example, an experienced shoplifter learns where most of the two-way mirrors are, who and where the store manager is, who and where the store detective is, what types of merchandise to expect to find, and how much money that merchandise will bring. With burglary, one rarely has such confidence in his or her knowledge of where the home owners are, when they might come home, when the police might drive by, what types of goods they may find, and how much money will be made from those goods.

Regardless of these uncontrollable variables with burglary, Floyd's perceptions of the risk of being apprehended were similar to those he held for shoplifting—next to nil. It became obvious from Floyd's description of his involvement in different types of crime that he was willing to try nearly any type to determine if he might like it.

After his brief and uncommitted stint with burglary, Floyd moved on to his second area of specialization—armed robbery.

A: Believe me, as soon as I first thought about armed robbery I did it. I never did armed robbery prior to that because I never considered them. Never thought about them. I got into armed robbery and I loved that. That was a real weakness to me there, right there, armed robbery.
Q: What did you love about it?
A: A lot of money.

Again, he assessed the risk of getting caught as miniscule, until he was sentenced to prison his first time.

A: Never in my life, until I got locked up for that fifteen years, did I ever consider being locked up. Never in my life.
Q: Did you know the penalty for armed robbery at that time?
A: No, never thought about it.
Q: How worried were you that you'd get arrested?
A: Never thought about it.

Although the harsh realities of being sentenced to prison and doing time educated Floyd to the real possibilities of arrest and imprisonment, he continued to believe that his skill would enable him to successfully commit crimes without further formal sanction.

A: From the age of eighteen until I got locked up, until I walked out of the penitentiary, until I got locked up this time, while I was out last time, the same thing. The same feeling. Everything was as if it never changed.
Q: So, are you saying you continued to think you wouldn't get caught and that you wouldn't be arrested?
A: Most definitely.

Floyd soon discovered that he was not untouchable. Before he went to prison, he had planned his crimes only minimally. After serving his first incarceration, he became a much more cautious criminal and one who was keenly aware of both punishment and various measures to avoid it. He began relying on his own skill at planning prior to committing armed robberies. He typically would watch the potential target for a few hours. His success then reinforced his belief that his planning was methodical and careful. He reported the following about the way he decided to commit an armed robbery as he watched the target and planned.

Q: As you considered doing the robbery, what did you think about?
A: The more I would think about it the more I knew that I wouldn't be caught for it.
Q: You weren't worried about getting caught?
A: No, not at all. Like I mentioned [earlier], my chances of being caught I felt was zero to one on a ten-point scale.
Q: What do you think accounts for that?
A: Confidence and just doing it before.
Q: Think of the way you weighed the possibility of getting caught against the benefits and—
A: I only thought of the benefits.

We see from the above that Floyd's confidence in his ability, reinforced by his previous success with armed robbery, enabled him to confidently make decisions to rob. This confidence, coupled with a calculus that continued to overfocus on the benefits, enabled Floyd to resolve an otherwise troublesome decision problem in a nonproblematic manner. He was virtually untroubled in his decision. He was not burdened by potential negative consequences and he believed in his own skill and planning. Hence the decision was an easy one.

During the interviews, Floyd was asked to describe the most recent crime he had committed and could remember clearly. He described in vivid detail a recent armed robbery of a store manager who had brought the store's money to the bank to place in the overnight deposit. Floyd's description of his decision making was articulate, especially compared to the individuals who found it difficult to explain their decisions and the calculus behind them. This victim was not randomly selected but was chosen because of the amount of cash that he possessed and because he was a manager—an individual in a position of authority.

Q: Tell me what kind of conversation you had with yourself about whether you should or you shouldn't.
A: I knew I should. And I was going to and it was going to be okay. The easiest money is armed robbery.
Q: Did you, at that time, think, "I could go to prison"?
A: No. You think about coming to prison about like you think about dying. Did I think about prison? No. I did not have no doubt in my mind I was good enough to do it and make it.

Again this illustrates how Floyd and other persistent offenders considered crime an occupation or profession. They considered themselves skillful and resourceful enough to successfully complete the task of their profession.

We went on to talk about risk perceptions and negative variables that he may have thought of during the decision to commit that particular armed robbery while he waited for the victim.

Q: Well, did bad thoughts actually enter your mind and then you put the thoughts out or did the thoughts not enter your mind?
A: No, they don't. They don't enter my mind, man.

Floyd and other non–drug-addicted persistent offenders relied heavily on their skill and past experiences. When they were faced with a decision to commit a crime after successfully committing a number of them and arriving at the opinion that they were good at their jobs, the decision was easily made. Their attention, mental conversation, and conversation with others (when others were included in the crime) focused on the logistics of the crime rather than other calculable risk-related factors. They did not deliberate over whether or not to commit it or focus on the potential for negative consequences from their actions. Those components of the decision problem were resolved, a priori.

Drug Addiction and the Persistent Offender

In *The Felon*, Irwin (1970) constructs "criminal identities" of various individuals involved in the commission of felonies.

Some of these identities proved useful in analyzing data and constructing criminal typologies for this study. One such identity of Irwin's is the "dope fiend," who represents those individuals who have had severe drug addictions for extended periods of time and whose life becomes dominated by drug use and addiction. Irwin also elaborates on several major themes of the dope fiend's world, which are "derived from the one dominant dimension—drug use" (1970: 16). The most important of Irwin's themes that relates to this study is that of committing crimes for the purpose of obtaining drugs. But stealing by the drug addict differs significantly from stealing by other offender types. For example, their stealing "tends to be pettier, less ambitious, less polished, more desperate, and more impulsive" (Irwin, 1970: 17). Irwin's study reveals that the extreme monetary cost of using large and regular amounts of expensive drugs and the physically debilitating effects of drugs make it nearly impossible for drug addicts to support their habits from legal earnings.

Those individuals in this sample who were severely addicted to drugs (see table 8.2) were predisposed to steal to support their daily addictions. The decision was not one of "should" or "shouldn't," but one of "must."

> A: I was off into drugs and I just didn't care. That's the kind of life I was living, so I was just out there and I was dealing with it, you know, survival or whatever.

In other words, they had to have drugs to function during the day.

> A: My mind kept saying, "Well you know, you've got to do this to get these drugs" and I would. If I didn't get the drugs, it'd make me sick. But when I get the drugs in me I'm okay, a normal person.

Stealing for most of these addicts represented an act of desperation, and required nearly no pondering, calculating, and resolving. Quite simply, given their addictions, they did what they defined as necessary to live. Their situation predisposed them to consider crime a viable alternative and when they decided for crime, the decision was situationally bounded. It was a "must" decision not only because they had defined the situation as such but also because of the very real and consequential physiological nature of their addictions. Deciding to and then committing crimes became an almost daily act. The decision was no longer a real deliberative decision but merely part of their routines. Committing crime became as routinized as injecting their drug. The decision was, in a sense, made for them by the very nature of their addictions. The following two individuals' statements well illustrate the almost total absence of calculative decision making.

A: A person as a drunk and an alcoholic, I found out now, I know now, there's no rational thinking of any sort. What you might feel is normal is totally abnormal. There's no rational thinking.

A: With drugs you don't rationalize. It's just a decision you make. You don't weigh the consequences, the pros, the cons. You just do it.

Because 44 percent of the persistent offenders in this sample were addicted severely to drugs or alcohol (see table 8.2), it proved worthwhile to distinguish characteristics of this particular offender type from those of the non-addicted persistent offender. The non-addicted were driven by factors that addicts were not and made decisions differently than drug/alcohol addicts.

Attention is now turned to the drug-addicted persistent offender. It will become clear when comparing this case study to the previous biography of Floyd, the non-addicted persistent offender, that certain offender characteristics and decision-making processes are unique to each particular type.

Hank: A Drug-Addicted Persistent Offender

Hank grew up as an only child living with his parents in a small town. He claimed that they were a solid middle-class family and that they "never went without."[6] He reported that his father worked as a fairly high-ranking county government official for a number of years during Hank's childhood and now owns his own business in the town. His mother manages a branch office for a state government agency. When Hank was in his mid-teens, his parents divorced and he lived with both parents—first with his mother and then with his father.

Hank grew up in a town that for years has had a statewide reputation for several illegal goods and services—moonshining, bootlegging, growing marijuana, and auto theft.[7] Citizens of the state and the community are cognizant of these kinds of illegal activities.[8] These illegal commodity suppliers are known by the community members, and many who work in illegal commodities also have legitimate jobs and are active in community affairs. Hank grew up in the presence of some of these people, and many of his friends and some relatives were actively involved. But, most important, this kind of behavior was not considered truly abnormal or deviant in this community. These activities are tolerated and accepted as more or less normal and nonthreatening to the community members and to the community's welfare.

Hank claimed that although he was aware of these types of operations and had friends working in illegal goods and services, he did not participate until his late teen years. In fact, he reported that he committed no crimes as a juvenile. This represents a significant departure from the development of criminal activity among the great majority of repetitive property criminals and especially among the non-addicted persistents.

Hank completed his high school education and never married. He was twenty years old the first time he was sentenced to prison. He was not jailed or incarcerated at any time prior to that. While in his late teens, he became involved in a "chop shop" operation; that is, he stole cars, stripped the original parts, and sold them. He claimed that he had always been exposed to this type of criminal operation by the older people involved in it. As he associated with these older people, he began to get more involved in the operation until he reached a management-like position where he paid people to steal for him. He was frequently involved in auto-theft operations and that was his specialty prior to his first incarceration.

Q: Then in that period from 1980 when you first came to the penitentiary, were you into crimes besides stealing cars?
A: Well, that's basically all it was.
Q: So how many cars do you think you were involved in stealing? How many cars and trucks?
A: Hundreds, because when you say every night and sometimes three in one night, you know, it don't take, you'd think that sounds like a big amount but it's not really when you do it on a steady basis.

From the above dialogue we learn that Hank was a frequent and repetitive offender who specialized at that particular period in his career in one crime—stealing and "chopping" cars. In other words Hank, like most persistent offenders, went through specialty changes or career changes in his larger criminal career but committed primarily one type of crime for a period of time before moving to a different type. Again, as we learned from Floyd, this study supports the concept of criminal specialization and represents a significant departure from earlier studies where criminals are portrayed as generalists who commit a vast array of different types of crimes and are uncommitted to a particular crime type (e.g., Petersilia et al., 1978; Chaiken and Chaiken, 1982).

As was discovered about other persistent criminals, Hank's major motivating force was money—quick easy money.

Q: Why do you think you stole cars at that time?
A: Well, it was for the money.

Hank represents a typical repeat offender because his perceptions of the potential benefits from committing crimes were unidimensional.

When asked about alternatives that he considered during the decision-problem resolution, Hank reported that at one time in his life, before he became addicted to drugs, he had considered and pursued legitimate alternatives, but then he soon opted for illegitimate.

Q: At that time did you see any alternatives that you could have done besides stealing cars?
A: I had had these summer jobs at night, you know. But, I'd done made up my mind at the time that I would just as soon have that easy money.

When questioned about his perceptions of the risks associated with that early criminal specialty, he reported that he operated with the assumption that if he were caught, the penalty would be pretty lenient. He, like most of these offenders, did not learn the penalty for this or other crimes until his first incarceration.

Later in life, through his association with people in the chop shop business, he began experimenting with different drugs and soon developed the same type of problem they had, a physiological drug addiction that eventually culminated in more serious legal problems and consequences, as he reveals in the following:

A: What got me in so much trouble . . . has been Dilaudid.[9]

Hank was not involved in burglary or armed robbery until his drug use increased to the point of addiction. His criminal involvement clearly paralleled his worsening drug addiction. After he became addicted to the drug Dilaudid, he began spending more money for drugs than he could make in the chop shop operations. Although acquainted with people who committed burglaries, he had never associated with them or involved himself in their criminal pursuits. He found himself, for the first time in his life, contemplating and then actively participating in burglaries.

Q: Why do you think you did that?
A: Simply for the drug money. I drifted with that crowd and they either shoplifted or did home burglaries or some kind of violation of the law every day. Whatever it is, you violate the law every single day on end.

When asked how he managed to actually make the decision to commit a crime, he responded typically for drug-addicted persistent offenders.

> Q: How did you manage to cope, how did you manage to—
> A: You know you're wrong, no matter . . . so you try not to think about it. You shake it off.

Like other repeat criminals, he claimed that he believed his capture was inevitable but continued participating in both the decision to commit crimes and the actual crime commission.

> A: You pretty well know you're doomed, you're destined. It's just a matter of time until the law enforcement stops you. I worried about it. You can't violate the law every day, two or three different ways a day and survive and get away with it. Eventually you'll stumble.

But his drug addiction, he claimed, both motivated and necessitated his continued criminal activities.

> Q: How did you mentally handle thinking that at any time you were going to get arrested?
> A: The drugs led the way. They made me think I could walk on water. I didn't judge anything at all. If I had just thought for a split second, but there wasn't no looking back, there wasn't no worries at the time. I decided to do it and didn't think about it till it was over. I wasn't raised up to steal.
> Q: Before you had the drug problem had you ever thought about breaking into somebody's house?
> A: No. I didn't have any desire to do that at all.

Hank was asked to describe the most recent crime that he had committed and could remember clearly. He chose to describe a house burglary that he had committed with another junkie. (Although persistents typically commit crimes alone, some drug-addicted persistent offenders, like Hank, commit some crimes with another person.) Hank and I methodically reconstructed the events, conversations, and his thoughts that preceded the crime. By so doing, we were able to discuss his thoughts about committing the crime and the factors within his decision to do it. He reported that he knew the morning of the burglary that he would have to commit some kind of crime that day to purchase drugs, and according to his definition of the situation, to survive.

> A: In the mornings you have to have [a fix] just to function as a normal person.

Other respondents who were questioned about their mood the day or night of the crime that they described to me reported that they were in "no particular mood," no different from any other day. Mood appears to have been a fairly insignificant variable in their decision to commit a crime. The drug-addicted respondents, however, typically reported they were feeling "bad," "depressed," "desperate," and "anxious about the next fix." Hank describes this mood:

> Q: What kind of mood were you in that day?
> A: I was in a bad mood, I felt bad. I hadn't done any Dilaudid that day and, like I said, you have to have it to function, period.
> Q: Typically, when you burglarized, were you in a bad mood?
> A: Normally in a bad mood or felt bad or I wouldn't have been doing it. It was a "have to" situation. You really had to have them physically.

Hank knew he would have to steal constantly for his addiction because he was not earning any legitimate money and he had come to rely on the quick, easy money that crime offered. He searched for a target on his own and then connected with another person with whom he had committed burglaries before. Their typical modus operandi was to drive around looking for suitable targets, or, as Hank said, "to make their opportunity."

When asked about the types of positive or negative factors he had thought about or they had talked about, he reported thinking about making easy money. They talked only of logistics and the division of labor for that specific crime, and did not talk about previous criminal successes or risk-benefit analyses.

> Q: Did you all talk about any negative things that you thought could happen to you?
> A: Well, no, you wouldn't talk about getting caught because the main thing is because you didn't want to get caught. So, you know, you more or less didn't want to talk about it or think about it.

He claims that he thought about negative consequences, such as arrest, imprisonment, and victim confrontation, but managed to temporarily block those worries from his mind. He typically relied on this neutralization technique to help face the impending danger and risk.

> A: You block out all those thoughts . . . you know it's wrong . . . you don't think about nobody but yourself, Mr. Greed. You just block them out for now. It's just a temporary block. You'll probably never be hooked on those type of drugs, but if you ever was you could see it clearly.

Hank was asked about alternatives to that crime that he had available to him or may have considered. He reported thinking of none.

> Q: Did you think about any alternatives to make money that day?
> A: No, that's the only way I knew at the time.

The only alternative that he reported thinking of during this particular period of frequent crime commission was at the heart of his criminal involvement—becoming drug free. He believed this alternative would someday be necessary for ending his criminal involvement, but at that time, it was an impossibility for him.

> A: I thought the only way to end my crime was to end the drug problem. See, the drug problem was the root of it all. That was the only alternative I had was to check myself in somewhere or leave town and get away from the drugs, period. But you go to a drug clinic and get out and you come back. Well, you're right back in the middle of it. Now how are you going to deal with it?

The majority of the drug-addicted persistent offenders, unlike the non-addicted, did not consider crime an occupation or profession. Rather, they viewed crime as an expedient way to fulfill their need—a need that most of them hoped was temporary. Driven by their needs, they committed types of crimes that they would not have considered otherwise. Also, their modus operandi was one of desperation, was more impulsive with little planning, and one where they constantly, as Hank said, "made their opportunities."

When Hank was asked to describe a specific occasion when he decided not to commit a crime, he was unable to do so. But like others who were unable to remember a specific incident, he did describe the most typical reason given for deciding not to commit a crime—instinct.

> Q: Instinct? What do you mean? Can you describe it?
> A: Well, it's a bad feeling, a feeling in the gut, like butterflies.
> A: So, it's not something you can point to?
> A: It's just something that, you know, comes to you, just something you feel yourself.

Earlier in the interview he had mentioned his recent and marginal involvement in the sport of stock car racing. I remembered this and began pursuing this topic with the hope of making "instinct" more concrete and generalizable as an experiential phenomenon. I thought of general nervousness common among performers and explored similarities between that and instinctive feelings about crime that was typical of both Hank and many others.

Q: Do you get butterflies before a race?
A: Oh, I get nervous every time. I get nervous, deadly nervous.
Q: Do those butterflies feel something like that intuition feeling you're talking about?
A: Well, in a way. But, they go away at the beginning of the race. They'll go away and you'll settle down, but the other, it'll stay with you.

Hank is atypical in one respect for the drug-addicted persistent offender. He was not involved in crimes as a young teenager. It was not until his late teens that he began stealing. This does not represent the majority's experiences. But, more significant is a pattern that does represent the majority's experiences among this offender type. The period of persistent and frequent crime commission was also the period of intensive drug addiction. Their drug addictions contributed significantly to their frequent participation in criminal activities.[10]

The Hustling Persistent Offender

As with the drug-addicted persistent offender, Irwin's analysis again is useful in delineating this type of persistent offender. Among his criminal identity types, Irwin identifies the "hustler." A significant component of the hustler's persona is "sharpness" of appearance and language. "The language-intellectual skills component is the ability to dupe, to outwit through conversation" (Irwin, 1970: 12). The hustler has developed a dichotomous view of those around him—those who take and those who are taken, and responds to this view by taking "the sensible course . . . to be one of those who take" (1970: 15). This expression is indicative of the hustler's lack of indecisiveness about committing crimes and is evidence of his beliefs about those around him and the social world.

The hustler, a subtype of the persistent offender, is one

whose mindset is to commit crimes on a nearly daily basis. The decision problem has become routinized as part of his daily activities, as has committing crimes, and is really no decision problem at all. Resolving the decision problem rarely follows the processes of theoretical decision making. Hustling is second nature to the hustler just as using drugs is to the drug addict. Malcolm X, a former hustler who became famous for empowering minorities and the oppressed, has the following to say about the life of the hustler:

> The . . . hustler is internally restrained by nothing. He has no religion, no concept of morality, no civic responsibility, no fear—nothing. To survive he is out there constantly preying upon others, probing for any human weakness like a ferret (Malcolm X, 1964: 311).

The majority of the persistent offenders, except for those who fit in the hustler subtype, appeared almost egotistical and were quite willing to talk of their exploits, their past accomplishments, and their lives. They were happy to volunteer information and rarely seemed guarded during the interviews. But the hustlers in this study were very well guarded during the course of the interviews. They were the most cautious, seemingly distrustful participants, and played their cards "close to their vests."

The hustler of the following case study undoubtedly was the most guarded respondent of the sixty. He clearly was suspicious of me and did his best to protect himself and his own interests. This guardedness was obvious during the interviews with all the hustlers and especially with Archie.

Archie: A Hustling Persistent Offender

Archie, who was raised in a large inner-city neighborhood, is thirty-nine years old, single, and the father of three children. He completed the seventh grade of school and made no attempts to obtain his GED. He has four siblings, none of whom has been in legal trouble. During Archie's childhood, his father worked as a custodian, making barely enough money for them to "get by." His mother at that same time was hospitalized periodically for emotional problems.

Archie's most stable period of legal employment across his lifetime lasted only nine months, shortly before his first prison incarceration, when he worked as a presser in a dry-cleaning business. During our conversation, he was asked about performing that type of work and what he thought about that type of job as a livelihood.

> A: Well, I seen nothing wrong with it, as long as I could make enough money to keep up with the cost of living—my standard of living. There wasn't nothing wrong with it.

This is indicative of the hustler's attitude about work and the work ethic. They certainly are not committed to it since they typically cannot earn enough money to live the lifestyle that they want and to which they become accustomed to with easy money from crimes.

Archie became involved in crime at the age of twelve or thirteen when he and his friends began shoplifting minor items that appealed to very young boys (e.g., candy bars, soft drinks). As they got older, they progressed to business burglaries. During the interview, I questioned him about the decision making of those early shoplifting and petty theft sprees.

> A: We didn't ever decide. We'd just take off to walking. It was a thing of kids just going to town all the time. You know, you go to town and wander around downtown and whatever you run into between town and back home, it was, "Come on, let's do this and do that." And then you're doing it. It wasn't no diabolical plot. Just spur of the moment.

He soon adopted a lifestyle and developed a mind-set which led him to steal to support his standard of living. He volunteered the following:

A: As you get older and see these same opportunities, I guess your desire for the taste of candy is going away.
Q: So when did it become bigger stuff?
A: When I started liking girls more or less, dating and cared about my appearance and the clothes that I wore.

This last comment illustrates his desire to look sharp in appearance, as Irwin (1970) found about hustlers.

He reported that when he was about age seventeen, he changed his approach to burglaries and his decision making about doing crime.

Q: You just said your approach to crime changed. How did it change?
A: I would say it changed to the fact that I would go at it more at the professional level. It was a serious thing now to me.
Q: If you had to say, "This is the reason I broke into places," what would it be?
A: I basically needed the money to keep up my standard of living. When I seen my standard of living falling I had to reinforce it with some currency.

Archie was sent to a juvenile reformatory twice between the ages of thirteen and fifteen and only four years later, at age nineteen, went to prison for burglary. He served one year. The next time he was incarcerated was when he was twenty-nine years old, again for burglary. This ten year period when he remained unincarcerated is unusual, especially for one who, I was firmly convinced, had not stopped committing crimes at a very high frequency—perhaps daily. After discussing his age at his first two incarcerations, I asked about his criminal activity during those ten years between prison sentences. Archie played the hustler in answering what he defined as a very sensitive series of questions.

Q: Did you burglarize during that ten year period?
A: During that ten year period, is that what you're saying? Did I burglarize in between that ten year period?

Q: Yeah, in that ten year period.
A: Did I?
Q: Yeah.
A: You're asking me that question? And you expect me to give you a straight answer?
Q: You don't have to answer it if you don't want to. It's just odd that if somebody was into burglaries there would be this ten year gap where they managed to get away with it, you know.
A: Well, no, it's not necessarily . . . it's a number of other things that you can do that work for you for a certain length of time and then when that particular thing is not working, you go into this thing that you rely on. Maybe a thing that you might feel that you're more experienced at.
Q: Did you do very many before you were caught?
A: Did I do very many? Now that's one question that I find it hard to come out of my mouth to even say that. You see what I'm saying?

Such sensitive questions put him on guard and he easily slipped into his view of the world—a view that led him to believe that I was attempting to corner him or entrap him in some way. He became elusive and refused to give a full answer to those most threatening questions.[11]

After serving one year for his second burglary conviction as an adult, Archie was reincarcerated a third time seven years later, again for burglary. He received a four year prison sentence, during which I interviewed him for this study. Archie claimed that he occasionally relied on different hustling specialties—gambling, selling marijuana, and buying and selling stolen merchandise. Again, he is typical for the hustler persistent offender in that, being streetwise, he was able to move easily from one hustle or specialty to another.

Archie was asked to describe the most recent and typical crime he had committed and could remember clearly. He related one specific burglary that he committed and his decision making prior to it. He was asked about the amount of time he had contemplated doing the crime.

Q: You had been thinking about that for awhile, then?
A: No, it's not like that. If you do things like that it's not a matter of thinking about doing it. You see valuable things as you go along day by day. It might be something that you can knock off when you might need some money. You spot things like that day by day as you go.
Q: How worried were you that you would get caught?
A: Not at all. I was rather bold. I didn't think about that much. [The worry] comes but you can wipe it away.
Q: How do you wipe it away?
A: You just blank it out.

Archie was also questioned about a specific time when he decided not to commit a crime. He, like many, was unable to remember one specific time, but remembered generally. He attributes those decisions not to commit a crime to instinct.

Q: What percentage of the burglaries that you thought about doing would you say that you didn't go through with, that you decided not to do?
A: I'd say 10 percent.
Q: For reasons like you're describing to me now?
A: Yeah, just bad feelings.

Archie, like most hustlers, knew the system and its ins and outs. Prison represented little threat to him, because he knew through experience that he could do the time. Hustlers, like most criminals, do not enjoy being incarcerated, but when that is the result of their decisions and actions, they accept it. Prison and the threat of prison are not components of their calculus and decision making before committing crimes. The threat of formal penalties certainly does not deter them from committing crimes.

The hustler is a criminal who calculates more carefully than the drug-addicted persistent or the low-rate sporadic offender (described below). The hustler, however, thinks little in advance about the logistics of doing the crime and does not rely on weighing the expected costs and benefits of completing the act, unlike what theoretical literature suggests. The hustler is always open to doing crime, always on the lookout and in effect decides first to do a crime and then searches for an amenable target. He searches for opportunities but targets selectively rather than jumping at the first opportunity that presents itself. This is not to say that he does not take advantage of opportunities, but his typical modus operandi is to first decide and then selectively choose a target.

The Sporadic Offender

The other decision-making type identified by this study is the sporadic or low-rate repetitive offender. These criminals had committed numerous crimes and had been incarcerated at least twice, but had not committed as many crimes with the frequency as the persistent offender. These less active criminals typically did not approach crime as a profession, a way of life, a status, or as a process by which they could obtain physical necessities (e.g., income or money for drugs to which they were addicted). These individuals typically were not addicted to a drug. In fact, only 7.7 percent were addicted to a drug at the time of their criminal activity, compared to 44 percent of the persistent offenders (see table 8.2). Sporadic offenders were relatively uncommitted to crime and rarely took the initiative or leadership role in crime commission. For example, only 11 percent of the sporadic offenders reported that they planned their crimes alone whereas 44 percent of the high-rate offenders reported they planned their crimes alone (see table 8.2). The low-rate sporadic offenders typically relied on one of several neutralization techniques to aid them with the decision to commit a crime (see table 8.4). The data also indicate that they continued to rely on the support of other, often older criminals to encourage them to decide for crime and to engage in it. The sporadic offenders also relied on alcohol as a neutralization technique to enable them to decide and then complete the risky activity. Of the sporadic offenders, 38 percent used alcohol when making decisions about committing crimes. These data indicate that sporadic offenders approached crime vastly differently from persistent offenders.

The alternatives that sporadic offenders considered

while resolving the decision problem of committing a crime are somewhat different from those considered by persistent offenders (see table 8.3). For example, 12 percent of the persistent offenders reported that they sometimes considered another crime to get the money they wanted. But, none of the sporadic offenders reported considering another crime. Rather, they were more likely to consider legitimate alternative actions such as borrowing money and seeking employment. In fact, 15 percent of sporadic offenders reported considering legitimate work as an alternative to the crime they were considering whereas none of the persistent offenders reported considering legitimate employment as an alternative.

Regarding perceptions of sanction threats, sporadic offenders expressed the most concern for both formal and informal sanctions for their criminal activities. They claimed to have worried about the possibility of arrest, imprisonment, and negatively altering their relationships with significant others. The risk component of the criminal calculus was given more weight by this offender type than by persistent offenders.

The following case study is of an individual, Abel, who is an excellent representation of the low-rate sporadic offender. He clearly was uncommitted to crime as a way of life, a profession, or a means to earn a living. His decision making was strongly affected by the influence of an older, wiser decision maker who had successfully committed a great number of crimes—his older brother. Abel's decision making was further affected by his use of alcohol as a neutralization technique, which altered him in such a way that he became an apprehensive yet willing participant in a few property crimes, one of which ended in murder. Abel claimed that he was involved in thirty-two different crimes—burglaries, shopliftings, selling stolen merchandise, and one armed robbery. His decision to engage in each of these crimes was made while neutralizing his fears and worries. But, he reported that he gave serious thought to the possibility of his arrest and incarceration, and the effect it would have on his personal life and his marriage. This assessment of various risks associated with crime commission is typical of the sporadic offender.

Abel: A Sporadic Offender

Abel grew up on a farm in a rural setting just outside a town with a population of 30,000. Abel's personality and characteristics fit those usually associated with rural farm boys. He was polite, concerned about others, and concerned about others' perceptions of him.

Abel attended public schools until age seventeen, at which time he had completed nine grades, a few in special education classes. Both of his parents were disabled and have been for many years. Abel has ten siblings, two of which have been involved in legal trouble. While living on fixed incomes with a thirteen member family, Abel claimed the family often had to do without and were in the lower social class. He worked erratically at only menial jobs, almost always as a laborer. He and his wife of seven years had their first child just before I interviewed him.

Abel was seventeen when he committed his first serious crime—a residential burglary with his older brother. He continued to commit burglaries, but only infrequently and with his brother, who not only strongly encouraged him but pressured him to commit crimes.

> A: My brother and them they'd get with me and stuff and they'd maybe say, "Yeah, we know where so and so place is and we can go and get some money and make a little money off of this." My brother . . . he's really the reason I'm in here today. He would always kind of encourage me.

He claims to have committed only ten to fifteen burglaries throughout his lifetime. They occurred infrequently and were distributed across the ten years of his life that he was marginally involved in crime.

At age nineteen he was incarcerated for the first time. He served three years for a rather serious charge, accessory to murder, that resulted from a botched armed robbery attempt. After his release from prison, he spent seven to eight years in the "free world" before he was reincarcerated for burglary. It was during his second incarceration that I interviewed him.

When Abel was asked about the decision to commit crimes he described his thoughts of both risks and benefits from crime. The possibility of losing his wife, the most significant other in his life, represented the most threatening informal risk he thought about prior to committing crimes. He claimed to have thought about her and their marriage prior to committing most crimes.

> A: I knowed I was going to get in trouble and I didn't want to be away from my wife. Just like I've laid a many a night and cried because I knowed that I had hurt my wife and she even cries every time she writes. Every week I get two or three letters from her and she writes stuff in there that makes me cry.

He reported that she described the various potential negative consequences from crime and encouraged him to cease his criminal activities.

> A: My wife, she told me, she said, "You're going to get locked up away from me. You're going to be gone for hard to tell how many years. You might liable end up getting killed sitting down there in them prisons because they's a lot of that goes on."

Abel and other sporadic criminals were those most concerned with the informal risks of disappointing, embarrassing, hurting, or being away from their significant others. Thus, his comments well represent sporadic offenders.

He claimed to have also thought about the risk of formal punishment prior to committing a burglary.

> Q: How worried were you that you would get arrested or sent to prison when you were doing those burglaries? Is it something that you thought very much about?
> A: I thought about it very, very much.
> Q: When did you usually think about it?

A Taxonomy of Criminal Decision Making

A: After.
Q: So how long after the burglary would pass until you would stop worrying about getting caught?
A: Somtimes it'd be about a month. I would lay in bed and think about it, think to myself. I'd lay on the bed with my eyes closed and just imagine a lot of times that the police was going to walk up any time and arrest me for doing so and so thing and take me and lock me up away from my wife.

From the descriptions and case studies of the persistent offenders we learn that they were rarely concerned with the threat of formal punishment. This is inconsistent with the perceptions of the sporadic offender. Sporadic offenders like Abel reported they often worried about formal consequences of their actions just as they worried about informal consequences.

The perceived benefits that Abel thought he would derive from burglary were typical benefits found among nearly all offender types, namely, money, excitement, and enjoyment. Except there is one significant difference here. Among the persistent offenders, the benefit of money represented the primary positive benefit obtainable from crimes. Most of these highly active offenders also reported the act was a way to have excitement but excitement was a latent benefit—a byproduct. Not so for sporadic offenders. Excitement and money were equally important benefits from crime, as Abel's words illustrate.

Q: When you thought about doing the burglaries . . . what were the benefits that you saw coming out of doing burglaries?
A: Well, when I was doing them I thought I was having fun and I thought I was making money for me and my family.

Abel, as did most offenders, relied on alcohol or drugs to neutralize his fears and worries. With his fears neutralized, he was able to participate in the risky decision and action.

A: I would always be a-drinking when I would do that stuff. It would always kind of boost me up and build my hopes up that I could do it. That booze and stuff, just like if you drink one can of beer you're going to want a second. You get that drunk you're going to want another one and it's going to keep on and keep on until it leads you on and on and then you're going to be out here doing this and that and then end up you're going to be sitting up here behind bars.

A second and very powerful neutralization technique of Abel's decision-making process was the influence of his older brother, who committed the murder during the armed robbery. This type of neutralizer was used almost exclusively by sporadic offenders (see table 8.4). Abel attributes most of his criminal involvement and legal trouble to this very important force in his life.

Q: Was your brother the one that initiated the stealing?
A: Oh, yes. He's really the reason I'm in here today. He would always kind of encourage me to go. He'd say, "Come on, let's go. Go over there where so and so is and we might make so much money," and we'd halve it. My brother, he would come by one day and he would talk to me. I'd a lot of times tell him, "No, I don't want to do this." And then, maybe the next day, he would come by and we'd sit around and talk about it and stuff and then we'd get out maybe a little drinking and something another and then's when we'd go do it.

When asked to describe the most recent crime that he committed and could remember clearly, Abel described the robbery and murder that he, his brother, and another accomplice committed. An atypical characteristic of this crime is that it was the only armed robbery that he claimed to have participated in. He was convinced to do the crime by his brother.

Q: What are the circumstances of that murder?
A: Well, my brother, he talked me into that. He said, "I know this man. He's got all kinds of money." Said, "Come on, we'll go over there and do this. They ain't going to be nothing happen."

A Taxonomy of Criminal Decision Making

His brother had committed armed robberies before and Abel relied on the expertise of this older, more experienced individual.

Q: Had he armed robbed before?
A: Yeah, he had did that a lot.
Q: And you never had?
A: No.
Q: What was your reaction when all of a sudden your brother said, "Hey, why don't we go over here and stick this guy up?" I mean, you'd never done an armed robbery before.
A: Well, it was, it was kind of a shock to me and I said, "Is anybody going to get hurt doing this?" And they said, "No. All we'll do is just go over there, draw the gun on the man, and tell him to set the money out. He'll set it out."

Relying on his brother's expertise and his previous criminal accomplishments, Abel was able to make the leap from committing burglaries to armed robbery.

Q: Tell me about the conversation that you all had, you know, what kinds of things were said, what kinds of things went through your mind.
A: I was scared. I said, "Bobby, I'll tell you what. We may get in trouble or we might end up getting killed by doing this," because I hadn't never did nothing like that. But he had and he said, "No, everything will be all right. You ain't got nothing to worry about."
Q: Did that convince you everything would be okay?
A: So I kindly figured to myself, well, I guess maybe it will be all right.
Q: So why did you think it would be?
A: Because he had got out of a lot of stuff and he had did a lot of stuff and had never got caught at it. I figured, well if he can get by with all them things I know we can get by with just this one thing.

He attributes his ability to finally decide to take part in the armed robbery on alcohol as a neutralization technique.

> Q: How did you manage to, thinking about all those things, how did you manage to do that crime?
> A: Well, one thing, well, that alcohol and stuff where I was drinking partly made me just go ahead and do it. Because when you get to drinking and you drink so much and you get so drunk, you'll do anything.

The calculus in this case, and characteristic of sporadic offenders, unlike other types discussed in this chapter, was not one-sided (i.e., risk was considered). The expected benefits, though, were discussed in a similar way that persistent offenders discussed them. Money and excitement dominated the positive expectations from crime.

> A: Well, we talked about when we got that money . . . we was going to do this and do that with the money. We was going to go and buy some nice cars and make us some hot rods and stuff out of them and build them up and make them mean and stuff.

Abel, like most sporadic offenders, felt guilty for committing crimes even at the time of commission. However, the sporadics were unable to rationalize away the moral and ethical dilemmas that they faced both when resolving a criminal decision problem and then afterwards. Not only did the sporadic offenders feel guilty but they also were keenly aware of the potential for informal sanctions from neighbors and friends and how the criminal actions might reflect badly on their families.

> A: I felt bad about doing that stuff. I felt bad about myself because I knowed people are looking, looking down on me saying, "Well there's nothing to him. Why, he ain't good for nothing."

Thus, sanction possibilities, whether formal or informal, played a significant part in the criminal calculus of these sporadic offenders.

Abel and other sporadic offenders were less committed to crime as a way of life and as an occupation. They often engaged in it for the excitement as much as anything. Abel, like other sporadic offenders, often used neutralization techniques while deciding to commit crimes. For example, they often were convinced to participate in crimes by other significant individuals in their lives. They relied on alcohol not only as a deadening device but also as an encouragement for committing crimes. Again, Abel claimed that alcohol helped give him courage while deciding to do crime and while doing crime.

Sporadic offenders are those who consider and worry about the risks of apprehension and formal punishment. Abel and other sporadic offenders reported that they occasionally thought about the police catching them and being sentenced to prison. They likewise reported some concern for risks of informal punishment. Reports of worries about their mothers and wives were common. Abel was not only worried about what effect his capture would have on his marriage but also what effect committing crimes might have on his marriage.

The decision to commit a crime for these offenders represented more of a decision than persistent offenders experienced. Deciding for crime often required some pondering, some going back and forth, with finally someone passing the bottle or talking it up, or both. For the sporadic offender, this was a serious decision and one that had the potential for grave consequences.

Conclusion

These typologies, accompanied with a case study of each, help conceptualize patterns and processes of decision making found among this population of repeat offenders. Each decision-making type both cognitively framed and resolved criminal decision problems in its own unique way. The interviews revealed that each type has different perspectives and opinions of crime commission and committed crimes very differently from the other types. Those components of rational decision making—alternatives considered, risk/benefit perceptions, neutralization techniques—are also unique to each decision-making type.

Whenever persistent offenders faced the decision to commit or not commit a crime, it was less of a decision problem or dilemma than for sporadic offenders. Persistent offenders daily functioned with the predisposition to commit crimes, so the decision was not one that required a great deal of deliberation. It was a given for them that they would commit crimes to meet their needs. Most had or sought no other alternatives to crime. The decisions that they believed required careful thinking and pondering were merely logistical (e.g., planning, casing, and target selection). They knew that theft offered quick, easy money, unlike legitimate work, and members of the subgroup of persistent offenders who were severely drug-addicted knew that in their drug-addicted conditions they would not be able to obtain and maintain legitimate employment. Thus, the decision to commit a crime for these persistent offenders was not a decision of "should" or "shouldn't" or one of calculation.

Early in this research, I questioned my confidence in the interviewees' accounts of their decision making, particularly because they were simplistic. But, I soon arrived at a logical explanation. Each participant showed difficulty articulating the atomistic steps and processes that they were pressed to explain. They had difficulty in analytically separating components of their decisions and had difficulty reconstructing thought processes during their decisions. When we compare their difficulty in reconstructing illegitimate decisions to the difficulty experienced by legitimate decision makers in reconstructing their decisions, this difficulty is easier to understand. Like criminal decision problems, many legitimate decisions are also risky (e.g., those involving substantial monetary investment, elective surgeries, participation in organized athletics). Those who resolve risky legitimate decision problems also experience difficulty in recalling specifics about their decisions to act. They are unable to provide accounts of alternatives to the decision and often make the decision while neutralizing fears of potential outcomes through drinking and conversation. Also, many legitimate decisions are made without knowledge of the possible outcomes and without calculation of perceived benefits and risks. Therefore, the difficulty in reconstructing criminal decision-problem resolution may be typical of reconstructing all types of decisions. It may well be that these cognitive human processes simply elude precise social science measurement, regardless of what we think we know about human beings and the processes of their decisions.

NOTES

1. Recent criminological literature has been flooded with debates over career criminals and criminal careers. Such debates often are over semantic differences rather than empirical differences in property offender typologies (e.g., Petersilia, 1980; Blumstein, 1982, 1986; Cohen, 1986; Gottfredson and Hirschi, 1986). Rather than inductively constructing empirical offender types that would ultimately benefit social scientists, policy makers, and society in understanding and treating repetitive offenders, researchers, it appears, often have settled for splitting hairs. Definitional and operational debates seemingly have done little to illuminate the central issue for deterrence researchers and policy makers, namely to explain the variance in perceptions of sanction threats among those who frequently commit crimes and those who infrequently commit crimes. After all the debates, it seems that we are little closer to the heart of the problem than we were before. From this pack of debative social scientists, a few have analytically situated the emergence of such criminal labels within a political and socioeconomic history (e.g., Kramer, 1982), and by doing so, have removed the use of criminal labels from their normally vacuous and insular setting. Kramer (1982) offers a conceptually useful understanding of the emergence of such labels. Criminal labels are created when there is a perception of increases in crime or in crime waves, and such labels focus attention on street crimes committed by the poor and powerless while diverting attention from both inequalities in social arrangements and "upper-world" crime.

Although research on the prevalence of crime (i.e., the proportion of the population ever arrested) shows that the majority of lawbreakers are not recidivists, public policy on crime has focused on those "chronic criminals" without questioning the social-structural conditions that may account not only for repetitive criminals but also for "large segments of the population [that] come into conflict with the law" (i.e., first-time offenders) (Tillman, 1987: 561). The point is, little research situates the emergence of criminal labels, repetitive offending, and one-time offending within a critical evaluation of social-structural conditions.

Our government maintains this focus by setting research agendas and funding research projects or public policy that focus on individual criminals rather than on social-structural explanations for property crime. This focus implicitly attributes our crime problem to a few "rotten apples" and leaves our socioeconomic structure unquestioned and intact. The final chapter of this book addresses social-structural conditions that contribute to crime.

2. "Lambda" as used in previous studies for constructing offender types is not to be confused with the more widely accepted use of the word. In that case, lambda is a statistic representing a bivariate relationship between nominal variables. Lambda as used here does not refer to a bivariate relationship but merely a univariate frequency or crime rate over time.

3. No matter how social science researchers choose to construct such typologies, a certain amount of arbitrariness cannot be avoided. Lambda as used in previous studies was defined based on informed yet arbitrary decisions of researchers just as I have resorted to here. The arbitrariness of making such constructs cannot be avoided, is not being criticized here, and should not necessarily be. Researchers are left to exercise caution when constructing taxonomies by using what we already know from previous theoretical and empirical works as we constantly work toward making sense of repetitive property crime as a social problem.

4. Early in the data analysis and typology-construction stages, lambda was to be used to help make sense of the frequency of offender crime commission. But, their self-reporting on their criminal activities across three specific age categories (i.e., juvenile, young adult, and adult) indicated that there undoubtedly was some overlap in their reconstructions of criminal activities for the age categories. Thus, it became less than clear exactly how frequently they committed crimes during a given age period, or during a particular stint in the "free world." With these problems in the data collection stages, I decided not to use lambda or rate, but chose to use frequency as a way of constructing offender types in this study. Frequency, for these data and their analyses, refers to "the number of occurrences of a particu-

lar category" (Theodorson and Theodorson, 1969: 162), that is, the number of various property crimes they committed. Thus, frequency, for this work, represents a raw number rather than a rate.

5. "Floyd" is a fictitious name. This name and all names used in this work have been changed to provide confidentiality and to "protect the guilty."

6. When I interviewed Hank the second time it was in his home. We met after he had finished his job for the day—a job with his father's small business. His home was small, but compared to other former prisoners' homes I had visited, it was very tidy, clean, tastefully decorated, and clearly showed signs of a comfortable middle-class lifestyle. Sea shells on a glass-top end table; a floor-model color television complete with VCR; and modern kitchen appliances including a dishwasher in an almond-decorated kitchen—it was not the typical ex-con's pad. Hank drove a fairly new pickup truck, told me of how he and his girlfriend enjoyed dining out and going to movies, and all about his recent hobby of racing cars on a dirt track. I had the opportunity to visit Hank's father's home on one occasion. He also had a very nice middle-class home with all the accoutrements. It was clear that Hank was indeed accustomed to a middle-class lifestyle.

7. The town was so widely known for auto-theft rings (a crime that Hank specialized in for a period of time) that a few years prior to this study, the CBS television news show "60 Minutes" broadcast a segment on the town and area's history with this type of criminal enterprise.

8. Although the residents of the town are fully aware of such illegalities flourishing in their community, they are tolerant of such activities for at least two reasons. One, the illegal enterprise produces a tremendous amount of cash income to those involved in the business. Two, almost everyone has a friend or relative involved in the business and they recognize it as necessary "bread and butter." This type of tolerance for illegal commodity production is similar to that among southeastern Kentucky and southern California marijuana-producing areas.

9. Dilaudid (medically known as Hydromorphine) is commonly referred to as a synthetic heroin, a prescription drug, that is commonly used by older junkies. It is a hydrogenated ketone of morphine and is as addictive. See chapter 3, note 4 for a more detailed explanation of Dilaudid.

10. There are researchers who discount the apparent relationship between drug addictions and criminal activity as too simplistic. There is disagreement over whether these individuals would have

committed crimes whether they were addicted or not and also whether these individuals use drug addiction as an excuse or justification for their crimes. Although these debates are important, they miss the most important point for understanding this relationship and for dealing with the increasing numbers of drug-related crimes. That is, regardless how much the addiction empirically contributes to their criminal activity, what is important is that these addicts define their addictions as important and as reason enough to commit crimes.

11. When Archie was interviewed the second time, after his release from prison, he continued to play his cards as close to his vest as he had during the first interview. We drove in a university car to a city park near his home and parked near a picnic table where we had planned to sit and talk. Upon seeing a group of young men not far away, he asked that I park elsewhere. When I asked why, he responded that they might think I was a cop and he did not want to be seen talking to me. During the interview, Archie responded very cautiously to sensitive questions, which is typical for hustlers. Since he denied committing any crimes during the nine months since his release from prison, he was questioned about whether he had thought about committing any crimes during that period.

Q: How long were you out before you thought about doing something wrong?
A: How long was I out before I thought of doing something? What do you mean wrong? Wrong in what way?
Q: You know, illegal.
A: Thought about it? What kind of question is that?
Q: It's a good, straight-forward question.
A: [Laughs] This ain't funny, not much. It's just you're asking me and the things that I know that I could be telling you.

Conclusion: What Shall Be Done?

9

The fundamental objective of this study was to understand the processes used by repetitive property criminals in making decisions to commit crimes. To this end, I used qualitative research strategies to learn from the once active repeat criminals their own recollections of decisions they had made to commit crime. Five primary themes were uncovered that raise critical questions for deterrence and decision-making research. They question the utility of shaping public policy by models of deterrence and decision making and indicate that just and well-informed public policies are long overdue. These five themes are explicated below.

First, these offenders typically decided to commit crimes by using one or more neutralization techniques that aided them both in their decisions to commit crimes and the actual crimes. The physiological and psychological effects of alcohol and drug use represent the most often used neutralizing technique among this sample. As a result, I believe this technique is a significant factor in explaining repetitive criminal decision making, not a causal explanation but a significantly telling one, or, to use Reiman's (1990) terminology, a "source" of crime. Those who relied on other techniques (e.g., conversation, deference to an older criminal and his influence, blocking thoughts of risk from their consciousness) did so to consciously and subconsciously avoid thoughts of risk associated with crime commission. Thus, although we have punitive policies to offset crime, individuals are perfectly able to neutralize their fears of punishment while engaging in criminal decision and actions.

Second, when the persistent criminals decided to commit crimes, few gave any thought to potentially negative consequences that might result from their actions. Not only did they not think about their chances of arrest, but also they gave little thought to their chances of imprisonment and no consideration to informal sanctions (e.g., the effects of their criminal activity on interpersonal relationships). Their failure to calculate negative outcomes, even simplistically, is incongruous with theoretical models of deterrence and decision making and questions the efficacy of deterrence policies on these individuals.

Third, by collecting data from the participants and using a qualitative methodology, we are a step closer to understanding the actual decision to commit crimes, perhaps as close as we can approach that moment, other than actually participating in the decisions themselves. As a result, patterns of decision making emerged and a taxonomy of decision making was constructed. The decision-making types explicated here (viz., persistent and sporadic) characterize individuals who are problematic for society, the judicial system, and countless numbers of individual victims whose lives they disrupt. These types likewise have important implications for our understanding of repetitive criminals, their reasoning processes, and deterrent effects on their actions.

Fourth, as a latent discovery, this study addresses the issue of criminal specialization. Earlier research questions whether repeat offenders are specialists in a given area of criminality or generalists who commit a wide variety of crimes. Early studies of criminal careers found that generalization is common among young criminals. Although they committed fewer types of crimes as they aged, they continued committing them opportunistically and as generalists (Petersilia et al., 1978; Petersilia, 1980). More recent studies of repeat offenders also found that they did not specialize in a particular crime type (Greenwood, 1982; Walsh, 1986). These findings are dissimilar to mine. Although the majority of these sixty offenders are not specialists in the sophisticated use of the word and are impulsive and disorganized when committing crimes, they typically specialized in one type of crime for a period of time, then moved on to another type of crime or specialty area. They occasionally returned to the original crime type but typically did not. Some reported they could adapt to long-range career changes by changing their specialties a number of times throughout their career. Only a few of the sixty reported shifting from one crime to another with the ease that Walsh (1986) found among his sample. Rather, this sample is more akin to that of Feeney (1986) who discovered that armed robbers considered burglary too risky and unpredictable, just as my participants did. For example, those in my sample who were specialists in armed robbery reported they did not commit burglary because there was (1) a lack of control of the situation; (2) a fear of being attacked by a home or business owner; (3) a dislike of the physical work of transporting the spoils; and (4) a disdain for the time and trouble involved in fencing the goods. Likewise, those who specialized in burglary generally reported one of the following aversions to armed robbery: (1) they wanted to avoid confronting the victim; (2) armed robbery was too dangerous; and (3) an armed robbery conviction could result in a long prison sentence.

A few individuals reported changing their specialty to avoid further arrests and severe prison sentences. They were aware that if they were arrested again for the same type of crime that they previously had been incarcerated for, there was a very real chance that they would receive a long prison sentence, since they would have established a pattern of committing that particular type of crime. They recognized the necessity of changing their "MO" to reduce their chances of rearrest and a long prison sentence.

In sum, my findings suggest that over time, offenders tend toward specialization. In their youth, these men committed minor offenses and also a wide variety of crimes. But as they matured and discovered by trial and error which crimes they felt comfortable with, they eschewed a variety of crimes and committed primarily one particular type of crime. Recent research confirms this by suggesting that specialization is an empirical given for some populations of criminals and that rejecting the concept of specialization is premature (Kempf, 1987).

The fifth major theme from this study indicates that not only did this group of offenders commit a disproportionate number of crimes, but their crimes may have been in part a result of their limited alternatives. Their long involvement in criminal activity is a result of both their objective conditions and their subjective interpretations of their conditions. Many truly were and are dispossessed individuals who lack the necessary assets to obtain legitimate employment and to earn a legitimate wage. Many likewise were severely drug- and alcohol-addicted to the point that they could not have maintained employment and certainly could not have earned enough to maintain their expensive drug habits. For some, their chances of establishing a legitimate lifestyle were better than most, but they had defined their situations in such a way that it had become futile for them to seek legitimacy as a way of life (e.g., a stable home life, legitimate employment, upward mobility). They became despondent and deduced that their only option was to continue committing crimes. Thus, both real material conditions and subjective definitions of their conditions explain their commitment to crime as a way of life and their lack of faith in legitimacy. This fifth and final theme is explicated in the next section.

Property Criminals as the Underclass

These offenders can be considered members of the underclass, the "truly disadvantaged" (Wilson, 1987), or the Marxian "lumpen proletariat." Using the generally accepted Marxian indicator of class—one's relationship to the means of production—the lumpen proletariat is that class that structurally is excluded from participating in the labor force. These sixty men had no relationship to the means of production. Similarly, recent research on those criminals that society selectively incapacitates shows that 65 percent of prisoners "had not finished high school, 64 percent had no job skills, over half had never been employed steadily, and 56 percent were not working at the time of their arrest" (Austin and Irwin, 1990: 16). Other studies mentioned throughout this work support these demographics on incarcerated individuals.

Reflecting their class location, these sixty criminals also communicated a consciousness indicative of the underclass or lumpen proletariat. They not only failed to recognize any antisystemic power that they and others like them may have had, but also lacked the insight to critically assess the legitimacy of the capitalist judicial system. Their decisions and statements about the system's legitimacy reflect the dominant ideologies that are reproduced socially and systematically rather than any semblance of antisystemic consciousness. For example, having been sanctioned two or more times formally and numerous times informally, nearly all sixty now conclude (unlike earlier in their lives) that predatory crime is morally and legally wrong and that criminals should be punished. And more surprising, most now believe that imprisonment is an appropriate form of punishment, without questioning policies that result in increasing numbers of people being incarcerated for longer times, and the inhuman method used by our society of caging individuals. Specifically, not one has critically evaluated: (1) the objective conditions that may have propelled them to repetitively commit crimes; (2) the very system that has punished them for their crimes; (3) the inequities of the capitalist judicial system; and (4) the inhuman treatment of systematically punishing people by imprisoning them. They do not challenge the dominant ideology that street crime poses a serious threat to individuals and that the solutions to criminality should be individual rather than social.

This evidence supports both Engels' (1892) and Wright's (1973) observations that crime is highly individualistic and disconnected from any conception of affecting social policy. These men's actions were poorly thought out, disorganized, and impulsive. Their targets were individuals and small businesses rather than governmental agencies, officials, or representatives of legitimate order.

The majority of these repeat offenders also gave little attention to the inequities that capitalism produces. This is a reflection of the class that they belong to—the underclass or lumpen proletariat—that class of individuals that is displaced by the logic of capitalism. Their class position reflects their lack of access to legitimate work, for they are not only dispossessed of ownership but also dispossessed of any relationship to the means of production or access to working as wage laborers. Their consciousness of a structure that displaces groups of individuals and punishes those who circumvent legitimacy to gain material wealth reflects a noncritical ideology. They have not developed any semblance of praxis or antisystemic strategy and have given little thought to the system that excludes them. They attribute their problems and situations to their individual faults and decisions. Both their exclusion and their lack of consciousness reflect their underclass position within the American class structure.

In the following section I discuss various recent public policies (e.g., selective incapacitation, rehabilitation, sentencing reform) that we have implemented to deal with predatory crime and the treatment of criminals such as these sixty. I show that such policies are troublesome for they offer little hope for any solution to the crime problem and if anything are dysfunctional for dealing with crime and criminals.

A Critique of Crime Policy

Doubtless, repetitive property criminals are considered "threatening" to Americans and to their property. The perception of the threat that they impose is a result of, among other things, political decisions and rhetoric. The focus by the media, the general public, and the criminal justice system is an individualist one where attention is given to a few "rotten apples" while greater social harms and threats, namely, governmental corruption and corporate harms to consumers, workers, and the environment, go unnoticed. But crime, whether corporate or individual, is a social problem that demands a social solution. Such social solutions have been diverse, to say the least.

Recent recurring "get tough" policies on crime and criminals have seemingly had little positive effect in reducing crime and have instead generated a whole new set of social problems. Increasing numbers of individuals are incarcerated, they receive longer sentences, prisons are filled beyond capacity, and growing numbers of parolees are left with the stigma of being ex-cons (or in Merle Haggard's words, they are "branded with a number on their name"). After all, selective incapacitation, mandatory sentencing, preventive detention, rehabilitation, and restitution are all dubious solutions to an American criminogenic society (Wright, 1985; Walker, 1985; Reiman, 1990).

Given that previous research has examined changes in the severity of punishment and found very little impact on individuals' perceptions and actions, deterrence-based policy may indeed be a misguided one that operates on false premises about those groups of offenders that are defined as threatening. Deterrence-guided social policy is not supported by this study and may be ineffective in reducing the numbers of crime, especially among the most active criminals, who commit a disproportionate number of crimes.

Incapacitative public policies are likewise ineffective strategies for reducing the societal toll of crime and for offering anything more to the criminal than a period of imprisonment. At the end of 1989, there were over 703,000 state and federal prisoners—a 115 percent increase in nine years (Bureau of Justice, 1990b; Austin and Irwin, 1990). And today, estimates are that the prison population is approaching 1.5 million (Johnson, 1991). The monetary investment of incarcerating increasing numbers of people for longer periods of time is staggering. If the rate of incarceration continues, Americans will spend twelve and a half million dollars per day just to keep pace with the demands for new prison space (Austin and Irwin, 1990). With the current conditions of prison overcrowding, the State's increasing role in socializing production costs, the various fiscal crises of the State (Block, 1981), the increasing costs of incarceration, and the State's continual problematic role in legitimating order, policy makers are having increasing difficulty justifying lengthening prison sentences. In fact, alternative strategies are finally being debated by individuals from all corners of the political spectrum.

Rehabilitation is currently a dead issue. The State's investment in rehabilitation programs resulted in convicts learning low-paying service or technical job skills. Critics of rehabilitation purport that there was never a full commitment by the State to invest large amounts of money and time into resocializing, educating, and training criminals to become contributing members of society (e.g., Martinson, 1974). For example, there typically have been few college courses offered in prisons and inmates are often required to pay their own tuition for correspondence courses. (If not so sad, this would be funny—uneducated, underclass individuals who earn about one dollar and fifty cents per day in prison are expected to pay a few hundred dollars for a single college course.) Rehabilitation ideologically endorses the pathological or individual faults approach to crime and criminals, which operates on the premise that criminals are sick and in need of treatment. Such policy ignores social-structural variables that may contribute to individuals' continued criminal involvement.

A liberal response to individuals who repeatedly commit property crimes is to somehow make the rewards from legitimate lifestyles and access to such rewards more appealing than they currently are. The logic is that criminals' desires to engage in crime would decrease as they increasingly pursued and obtained material goals through socially acceptable and increasingly attractive means. This is a naive position since the majority of individual street criminals are excluded from and hence have little access to a secure, legitimate lifestyle, no matter how appealing this lifestyle might be or become. Thus, a liberal approach seems a dubious one for dealing with the social problem of crime among a problematic population of committed criminals.

A totally different approach to crime and criminals is a Marxist or critical approach. This perspective emphasizes the need for a humanistic, people-oriented criminal justice system that ideally functions within a socialist State. Therefore, for Marxists, an appropriate agenda for implementing truly "social" public policies is to work toward a socialist revolution (whether immediate or eventual). Marxists believe that as a result, crime, especially property crime, would be reduced.

As appealing as such an agenda is, Marxists realize there is much systemic resistance to the implementation of these policies. They specifically realize that (1) the U.S. is a major capitalist world power; (2) the State in our society must function as a capitalist State to preserve the larger economic system; and (3) the logic of capital naturally results in inequalities rather than an equitable, people-oriented society. As we think about and work toward solving the problems that repeat offenders pose and humanizing our society, I offer some policy suggestions that are humanist, Marxist, and that could be adopted within a pre-socialist State. I recognize that some are contradictory to the logic of capital, to the capitalist State, and to the objectives of today's U.S. capitalism. The introduction of such policies would result in a reduction of profit maximization within an economic system that thrives on just that. I also realize that by making such policy suggestions, I provide the ammunition that ultimately could benefit the State to further legitimize the existing system. I could be criticized for acting in a way that is contrary to a peoples' revolution and in a way that is beneficial to the State's further control.

As a response to such possible accusations, I believe there are at least two courses of action available to those interested in humanizing the criminal justice system specifically and society generally. First, we could do nothing and allow further dehumanizing social policies to prevail. Some orthodox Marxists might recommend this course of action for, they believe, it would further polarize classes, lead to a worsening of social conditions, and make the ground fertile for a socialist revolution. Second, we could implement policies whose objective is to derationalize capitalist society (Weber, 1978), the State, and the criminal justice system. This is a difficult task, for it leaves the structure unaffected and unchallenged. Some less orthodox Marxists would, nonetheless, recommend such a course of action, for it does not forsake an ideological commitment to socialism and at the same time, it addresses the immediate needs of society, namely, addressing inequalities in wealth and health, changing the foci of criminal definitions, and decriminalizing actions presently labeled "criminal." My own position is a historical materialist one with faith in the imminent arrival of socialism. But until that time, the State could conceivably commit itself to the good of the public rather than to the good of the minority—the privileged class—while at the same time reducing the societal toll of crime.

With an understanding of these offenders, their class location and consciousness, and previous and current crime policies, I offer the following policy suggestions that could be used to make this society a more just and humane one and to address the problem of a chronic underclass in this society, the criminality that arises from such a class, and the many prisons that are overfilled with individuals from that class. After all, the adage "Poverty is the mother of crime" can't be all wrong. I am convinced that structural conditions account for some repeat criminality, that is, individuals who commit themselves to a life of crime. We need public policies that are well informed and that offer structural solutions to the predatory crime problem. Such policies, in embryonic form, are addressed in the final pages of this chapter. These policies represent a departure from social-psychological issues addressed throughout this work and are much broader in scope. The social-psychological process of decision making, as important as it is, must be situated within the structure that individuals function within to understand their options, the factors that propel them to commit crime, and the relationship between their drug addictions and their repetitive crime commission. Thus, policies suggested in the remainder of this work depart from subjective interpretations of property offenders and crime per se and focus on macrosociological processes that work in shaping the destinies of individuals, including property offenders.

Wealth Redistribution

Recent studies indicate that wealth is being squeezed into fewer and fewer hands. In the past three decades, we

Conclusion: What Shall Be Done?

have witnessed ever more capital and income becoming possessions of fewer numbers of individuals who occupy the upper strata in the class structure. For example, "the top one-half of 1 percent of American families . . . now own 44 percent of America's wealth and business assets (up from 31 percent in 1963) . . . and the bottom 45 percent [of Americans possess] less than 2 percent" (Gorman, 1989: 171). The trend for income possession shows the situation is becoming just as polarized. Thus, policies that reverse this trend are desperately needed to make income and capital accessible to the populace and not simply one-half of one percent—the super rich. A policy by which wealth is redistributed through a revised, progressive tax system should be adopted. The State could take in greater revenue by overhauling the income tax system to tax both individuals and businesses. With this increased revenue, the State could initiate domestic policies to redistribute wealth so that those who are presently dispossessed are no longer. Thus, the State could take the initiative not only in making this a more equitable society but also in countering a known source of crime—poverty (Reiman, 1990). Reiman's words are an indictment of our society's unwillingness to eliminate poverty, when such an accomplishment is possible.

> We are long past the day when we could believe that poverty was caused by forces outside human control. Poverty is "caused" by lack of money, which means that once a society reaches a level of prosperity at which many enjoy a relatively high standard of living, then poverty can be eliminated or at least significantly reduced by transferring some of what the "haves" have to the "have-nots." In other words, regardless of what caused poverty in the past, what causes it to continue in the present is the refusal of those who have more to share with those who have less (1990:74).

Undoubtedly, any effect on poverty by implementing wealth redistribution policies would be a long process, but knowing that poverty is strongly related to property crime, such measures seem to be a worthwhile and long overdue social investment.

Educational Reforms

Primary and secondary educational systems should be made more equitable by eliminating the implicitly unequal policy of funding local schools based on local tax revenues. This would eliminate inferior educational systems for impoverished groups that typically are segregated from middle- and upper-class communities. The federal government could play a larger role in determining that public schools are funded on an equal basis.

Likewise, higher education should be state subsidized to make it accessible to every qualified student rather than the middle and upper classes. By initiating this policy, the State could immediately address the age-old problem of multigenerational poverty by allowing the young and future generations another avenue by which to exit the ranks of the poor. This means that those classes whose populations engage in crime due to their limited opportunities would ultimately find new opportunities available.

Empowerment ideologies should be essential components of education nationally (e.g., a Paulo Freire, 1981, approach). Much like empowerment programs already very active (e.g., the Highlander Research Center), such programs in education would enable students to learn through a culture of critical discourse (Gouldner, 1979) while at the same time rethink those issues that are important for living communally rather than competitively. Such policies would enable students to take greater control of their lives and destinies rather than live with the fear of continual dependency, especially those groups of individuals who presently have little stake in conformity. Empowerment programs do work well in some areas but would be accessible to greater numbers of people if they became official state policy. This policy would work toward ideologically and materially freeing groups of individuals who, at this time, have few options other than crime available to them.

Structural Changes in the Criminal Justice System

The State should take an active role in refocusing criminal definitions and the public's interest in those crimes that are the most harmful socially (e.g., corporate wrongdoings) and divert attention from street crime and criminals. Such a policy would direct attention toward where it is lacking and also toward actions that cause grave social harm. Yearly estimates continually indicate that corporate violations of regulatory laws cost us, as a society, more in lost dollars and human lives than all property and violent crimes (Reiman, 1990). Focusing on such actions would signal the beginning of a policy aimed at lessening such grave consequences to our society.

Further, drug use and victimless crimes (e.g., drunkenness, gambling, public order laws, vagrancy, juvenile delinquency, sexual behavior) should be decriminalized, as has been proposed repeatedly by various progressive individuals and groups (e.g., Morris and Hawkins, 1970; Walker, 1985; Trebach, 1987; Reiman, 1990). Despite such enlightened calls, in the past few years most states and the federal government have implemented mandatory sentencing for drug law violators, which means that not only are greater percentages of individuals convicted for drug cultivating, manufacturing, and sale going to prison but also that they are being sentenced to much longer sentences than just a few years ago. For example, in 1989, of the individuals sentenced to federal prison, 44 percent were for drug charges, a drastic increase from just ten years earlier (Drug Trafficking, 1989). The combination of these two policies (lock 'em up and lock 'em up longer) results in our prisons filling up and remaining filled with individuals who have caused very little social harm and who pose very little threat. By decriminalizing such behavior, the various components of the criminal justice system would be freed up from dealing with such minor actions and could then channel their resources into preventing, detecting, and apprehending individuals and organizations involved in more socially harmful activities. Also the policy of treating addiction and the addict as criminal should be discontinued. Individuals opposed to decriminalization as a partial solution to the crime problem suggest that addict-criminals would commit crimes anyway, regardless of whether or not they were addicted. This may be true, but we know that addiction and the illegal status of drugs in this country place addicts in positions where they must steal to purchase their overpriced illegal drugs and the other necessities of life. This relationship is not something that we guess at or intuit. Rather it is an empirical fact and a relationship that we can speak of with much confidence (a rarity in the social sciences). Given this knowledge, it seems only reasonable to alter our public policy on drugs in the hope that the frequency of property crime commission would be reduced and that individuals who choose to use addictive drugs could do so affordably without the need to commit crime and without the effects of the "criminal" label applied to them and their activities.

The criminal justice system itself is in need of rehabilitation and the agendas of the police, courts, and corrections need changing (Maguire, 1988; Reiman, 1990). For example, the role of the police could be changed to one of caretaker rather than one of law enforcer. Recent survey research with progressive criminologists indicates they believe the police could be given "helping roles" or converted into "social workers," whose social sensitivity "rather than technical abilities like marksmanship" is promoted (Maguire, 1988: 140). In effect, the police should be modeled less after the military and more after a social service organization that is an integral service to the community. As long as the police are modeled after the military and as long as we define their jobs as soldiers in a war on crime (or drugs), they will respond in kind to their labels and missions.

The court's concern should be with social harm. Individuals and organizations that cause social harm should be those brought to trial in a court. Thus, consumer fraud, environmental pollution, and governmental wrongdoings would be treated by criminal courts rather than simply by regulatory agencies. Likewise, policies that provide indigent populations with counsel do not assure them of competent counsel, for we know that "free" representation does not always translate to "equal" representation. Individuals who currently are the most often prosecuted in criminal courts (i.e., the underclass) should be allowed to claim monies to hire an attorney of their choice through a "national legal insurance program" (Maguire, 1988: 142).

The role of prisons could be greatly diminished as we rely

on less restrictive and oppressive means for punishing. As a result, the building of more prisons would become unnecessary and we could use those monies on much-needed domestic spending as a social investment (Scull, 1984). An experience in prison as it currently operates contributes to an individual's continued involvement in crime and is recognized as a source of crime (Reiman, 1990). Doubtless, dangerous violent offenders must be incapacitated, but the countless numbers of drug law violators and petty property offenders that we imprison could be dealt with in more humane and less costly ways. Recent research shows that 52 percent of the national prison population is serving time for petty crimes (Austin and Irwin, 1990). Progressive criminologists have suggested that those violent individuals that we incapacitate should continue to be incapacitated, with one exception. There is a point in most criminals' lives when they slow down and refrain from engaging in crime. With this in mind, rather than incarcerating a violent offender for his or her entire life, hold him or her only until that point when most offenders slow down and become less likely to participate again in crimes (Maguire, 1988). These suggestions are humanistic approaches to policy changes regarding our criminal justice system—a system much in need of rehabilitation.

Conclusion

Crime is not an isolated phenomenon but is meticulously and historically woven in the fabric of this society. We have experienced about the same levels of violent crime since the 1930s (regardless of what politicians have said about periodic "crime waves") and little flux in property crimes over the past fifteen years (Wright, 1985). As a result, an explanation for crime and its pervasiveness surely lies in areas other than the uncontrollable urges of a few amoral criminals. Although both conservative and liberal programs may be intuitively appealing, they have proven ineffective both in reducing the level of predatory crime and making this a more humane society to live in. Recent research shows that this society is "tough" on criminals, that the chances of apprehending more criminals are very slim, and that offenders typically do not respond in the ways that we want when we attempt to manipulate their behavior through both deterrence and rehabilitation policies (Walker, 1985).

How can crime be lessened and how can we deal with populations of repeat offenders? I am convinced that we can potentially reduce crime by implementing the policies I describe here since the vast majority of property criminals are members of the underclass. By adopting such policies, the quality of all our lives would greatly appreciate, especially the quality of life among the underclass. These policies, in part, may reduce the need for committing crime that currently exists in this profit-motivated, individualist society. And as a result, we should end up investing less money on crime control and containment than we currently do. We know that the various criminal justice policies and programs that have been initiated throughout our short history have failed miserably, for we have been unable to counter crimes and individuals' decisions to engage in crime. The progressive policies that I suggest are departures from the more common, simplistic, band-aid, quick-fix solutions. These policies speak to fundamentally important issues that I believe are necessary to address if we indeed wish to reduce property crime and the threat that it poses.

References

Agar, M. H.
1977 "Ethnography in the streets and the joint: A comparison." Pp. 142–56 in Robert S. Weppner (ed.), *Street Ethnography*. Beverly Hills, CA: Sage.
Akers, Ronald L.
1977 *Deviant Behavior: A Social Learning Approach*. Belmont, CA: Wadsworth.
Akerstrom, Malin
1985 *Crooks and Squares*. New Brunswick, NJ: Transaction.
Andenaes, Johannes
1974 *Punishment and Deterrence*. Ann Arbor, MI: University of Michigan Press.
Austin, James and John Irwin
1990 *Who Goes to Prison?* San Francisco: National Council on Crime and Delinquency.
Bailey, William C.
1975 "Murder and capital punishment." Pp. 408–20 in William J. Chambliss (ed.), *Criminal Law in Action*. Santa Barbara, CA: Hamilton.
Bailey, William C. and Ronald W. Smith
1972 "Punishment: Its severity and certainty." *Journal of Criminal Law, Criminology, and Police Science*. 63: 530–39.

Beccaria, Cesare B.
1963   *On Crimes and Punishments*. Indianapolis: Bobbs-Merrill.
Beck, Allen J. and Bernard E. Shipley
1987   "Recidivism of young parolees." *The Criminal Justice Archive and Information Network* Fall: 1 & 3.
Beck, Richard A. and Joseph M. Adams
1970   "Establishing rapport with deviant groups." *Social Problems* 18: 102–18.
Becker, Gary S.
1976   *The Economic Approach to Human Behavior*. Chicago: University of Chicago Press.
1968   "Crime and punishment: An economic approach." *Journal of Political Economy* 76: 169–217.
Becker, Gary S. and William M. Landes
1974   *Essays in the Economics of Crime and Punishment*. New York: National Bureau of Economic Research.
Becker, Howard S.
1986   "Studying practitioners of vice and crime." Pp. 137–57 in *Doing Things Together: Selected Papers*. Evanston, IL: Northwestern University Press.
1970   "Conventional crime: Rationalizations and punishments." Pp. 329–39 in *Sociological Work: Method and Substance*. Chicago: Aldine.
1963   *Outsiders*. New York: The Free Press.
Bennett, Trevor and Richard Wright
1984a   "What the burglar saw." *New Society* 2: 162–63.
1984b   *Burglars on Burglary*. Hampshire, UK: Gower.
Bentham, Jeremy
1970   *An Introduction to the Principles of Morals and Legislation*. London & New York: Methuen.
Best, Joel and David F. Luckenbill
1982   *Organizing Deviance*. Englewood Cliffs, NJ: Prentice-Hall.
Block, Fred
1981   "The fiscal crisis of the capitalist state." *Annual Review of Sociology* 7: 1–27.
Blumstein, Alfred
1986   *Criminal Careers and Career Criminals*, Vol. 1. Washington, DC: National Academy Press.
1982   The Duration of Adult Criminal Careers. Final Report to the National Institute of Justice. Pittsburgh: Carnegie-Mellon University Press.

Blumstein, Alfred, Jacqueline Cohen and David P. Farrington
1988a   "Criminal career research: Its value for criminology." *Criminology* 26: 1-35.
1988b   "Longitudinal and criminal career research: Further clarifications." *Criminology* 26: 57-74.

Blumstein, Alfred and Jacqueline Cohen
1987   "Characterizing criminal careers." *Science* 237 (28): 985-91.

Blumstein, Alfred, Jacqueline Cohen and Daniel Nagin
1978   *Deterrence and Incapacitation: Estimating the Effects of Criminal Sanctions on Crime Rates.* Washington, DC: National Academy of Sciences.

Braverman, Harry
1974   *Labor and Monopoly Capital: The Degradation of Work in the Twentieth Century.* New York: Monthly Review Press.

Brown, Ivan D.
1981   "The traffic offence as a rational decision." Pp. 203-22 in Sally M.A. Lloyd-Bostock (ed.), *Psychology in Legal Contexts: Applications and Limitations.* London: Macmillan.

Brown, William and Morgan Reynolds
1973   "Crime and punishment risk implications." *Journal of Economic Theory* 6 (5): 508-14.

Buckle, Abigal and David P. Farrington
1984   "An observational study of shoplifting." *British Journal of Criminology* 24: 63-73.

Bureau of Justice Statistics
1990a   "Crime and the nation's households, 1989." *Bureau of Justice Statistics Bulletin* (September). Washington, DC: U.S. Department of Justice.
1990b   "Prisoners in 1989." *Bureau of Justice Statistics Bulletin* (May). Washington, DC: U.S. Department of Justice.
1990c   Personal telephone call to Bureau of Justice Statistical Clearing House on September 5.
1989   "Recidivism of prisoners released in 1983." *Bureau of Justice Statistics Bulletin* (April). Washington, DC: U.S. Department of Justice.

Burgess, Robert G.
1982   *Field Research: A Sourcebook and Field Manual.* London: George Allen and Unwin.

Carroll, John S.
1982   "Committing a crime: The offender's decision." Pp. 49-67 in Vladimir J. Konecni and Ebbe B. Ebbesen (eds.),

The Criminal Justice System: A Social-Psychological Analysis. San Francisco: W. H. Freeman.

1978 "A psychological approach to deterrence: The evaluation of crime opportunities." *Journal of Personality and Social Psychology* 36: 1512–20.

Chaiken, Jan M. and Marcia Chaiken
1982 Varieties of Criminal Behavior. Report to the National Institute of Justice. Santa Monica, CA: Rand Corporation.

Chambliss, William J.
1972 *Box Man: A Professional Thief's Journey.* New York: Harper & Row.
1966 "The deterrent influence of punishment." *Crime and Delinquency* 12: 70–5.

Chiricos, Theodore and Gordon P. Waldo
1970 "Punishment and crime: An examination of some empirical evidence." *Social Problems* 18: 200–217.

Clarke, Ronald V. and Derek B. Cornish
1985 "Modeling offenders' decisions: A framework for research and policy." Pp. 147–85 in Michael Tonry and Norval Morris (eds.), *Crime and Justice: An Annual Review of Research,* Vol. 6. Chicago: University of Chicago Press.

Clarke, Ronald and Tim Hope
1984 *Coping With Burglary.* Hingham, MA: Kluwer/Nijhoff.

Clinard, Marshall B. and Richard Quinney
1967 *Criminal Behavior Systems: A Typology.* New York: Holt, Rinehart and Winston.

Cloward, Richard A. and Lloyd E. Ohlin
1960 *Delinquency and Opportunity.* New York: The Free Press.

Cohen, Jacqueline
1986 "Research on criminal careers: Individual frequency rates and offense seriousness." In Alfred Blumstein, Jacqueline Cohen, Jeffrey Roth, and Christy Visher (eds.), *Criminal Careers and "Career Criminals,"* Vol. 1. Washington, DC: National Academy Press.

Cook, Phillip J.
1980 "Research in criminal deterrence: Laying the groundwork for the second decade." Pp. 211–68 in Vol. 2 of Norval Morris and Michael Tonry (eds.), *An Annual Review of Research.* Chicago: University of Chicago Press.

Cornish, Derek B. and Ronald V. Clarke
1987 "Understanding crime displacement: An application of rational choice theory." *Criminology* 25: 933–47.

Cressey, Donald R.
1973   *Other People's Money*. Montclair, NJ: Patterson Smith.
Douglas, J.
1980   *Introduction to the Sociologies of Everyday Life*. Boston: Allyn and Bacon.
1989   Drug Trafficking: A Report to the President compiled by the U.S. Attorneys and the Attorney General of the United States. Washington, DC: U.S. Department of Justice.
Ehrlich, Isaac
1975   "The deterrent effect of capital punishment: A question of life and death." *American Economic Review* 65: 397–417.
1973   "Participation in illegitimate activities: A theoretical and empirical investigation." *Journal of Political Economy* May: 521–65.
Ellen, R. F.
1984   *Ethnographic Research: A Guide to General Conduct*. London, UK: Academic Press.
Engels, Frederich
1943   *The Condition of the Working Class in England*. London: S. Sonnenschein & Company, translated by Florence K. Wischnewtzky from the first publication, March 1892.
Erickson, Maynard L., Jack P. Gibbs, and Gary F. Jensen
1977   "The deterrence doctrine and the perceived certainty of legal punishments." *American Sociological Review* 42: 305–17.
Farrington, David P.
1983   *Further Analysis of a Longitudinal Survey of Crime and Delinquency*. Washington, DC: National Institute of Justice.
1979   "Longitudinal research on crime and delinquency." Pp. 289–348 in Norval Morris and Michael Tonry (eds.), *Crime and Justice: An Annual Review of Research*. Vol. 1. Chicago: University of Chicago Press.
Feeney, Floyd
1986   "Robbers as decision-makers." Pp. 53–71 in Derek B. Cornish and Ronald V. Clarke (eds.), *The Reasoning Criminal*. New York: Springer-Verlag.
Firey, Walter
1969   "Limits to economy in crime and punishment." *Social Science Quarterly* 50: 72–77.
Flanagan, Timothy and Katherine M. Jamieson
1988   *Sourcebook of Criminal Justice Statistics, 1987*. Washington, DC: U.S. Department of Justice.

Frazier, Charles E.
1978 "The use of life histories in testing theories of criminal behavior." *Qualitative Sociology* 2: 122–42.
1976 *Theoretical Approaches to Deviance*. Columbus, OH: Charles E. Merrill.

Frazier, Charles E. and Thomas Meisenhelder
1985 "Criminality and emotional ambivalence: Exploratory notes on an overlooked dimension." *Qualitative Sociology* 8: 266–84.

Freeman, C. R.
1980 "Phenomenological sociology and ethnomethodology." Pp. 113–54 in J. Douglas, P. Adler, A. Fontana, C. R. Freeman, and J. Kotanba (eds.), *Introduction to the Sociologies of Everyday Life*. Boston: Allyn and Bacon.

Freire, Paulo
1981 *Pedagogy of the Oppressed*. New York: Continuum.

Gardner, Howard
1985 *The Mind's New Science*. New York: Basic Books.

Geerken, Michael R. and Walter R. Gove
1975 "Deterrence: Some theoretical considerations." *Law & Society Review* 9: 497–513.

Gibbons, Don C.
1979 *The Criminological Enterprise*. Englewood Cliffs, NJ: Prentice-Hall.

Gibbs, Jack P.
1981 *Norms, Deviance and Social Control Conceptual Matters*. New York: Oxford Press.
1968 "Crime, punishment, and deterrence." *Southwestern Social Science Quarterly* 48: 515–30.

Givan, Richard E.
1988 "Outlaws who are in: Criminals who become folkheroes." Paper presented to the American Popular Culture Association, New Orleans, LA, Spring.

Glaser, Barney
1978 *Theoretical Sensitivity*. Mill Valley, CA: Sociology Press.

Glaser, Barney and Anselm L. Strauss
1967 *The Discovery of Grounded Theory: Strategies for Qualitative Research*. Chicago: Aldine.

Glassner, Barry and Cheryl Carpenter
1985 "The feasibility of an ethnographic study of adult property offenders." Unpublished report prepared for the National Institute of Justice.

Goffman, Erving
1963 *Stigma: Notes on the Management of Spoiled Identity*. Englewood Cliffs, NJ: Prentice-Hall.
Goldberg, Lewis R.
1970 "Man versus model of man: A rationale, plus some evidence, for a method of improving on clinical inferences." *Psychological Bulletin* 73: 422–32.
Gordon, David M.
1973 "Capitalism, class, and crime in America." *Journal of Research in Crime and Delinquency* 3:123–37.
Gordon, David M., Richard Edwards, and Michael Reich
1982 *Segmented Work, Divided Workers*. Cambridge: Cambridge University Press.
Gorman, Robert A.
1989 *Yankee Red: Nonorthodox Marxism in Liberal America*. New York: Praeger.
Gottfredson, Michael R. and Travis Hirschi
1986 "The true value of lambda would appear to be zero: An essay on career criminals, criminal careers, selective incapacitation, cohort studies, and related topics." *Criminology* 24: 213–33.
Gouldner, Alvin W.
1979 *The Future of Intellectuals and the Rise of the New Class*. New York: Oxford University Press.
Grasmick, Harold G.
1985 "The application of a generalized theory of deterrence to income tax evasion." Paper presented at the Law and Society Meeting, June 7.
Grasmick, Harold G. and George J. Bryjak
1980 "The deterrent effect of perceived severity of punishment." *Social Forces* 59: 471–91.
Grasmick, Harold G. and Herman Milligan, Jr.
1976 "Deterrence theory approach to socioeconomic/demographic correlates of crime." *Social Science Quarterly* 57: 608–17.
Green, Gary S.
1985 "General deterrence and television cable crime: A field experiment in social control." *Criminology* 23: 629–45.
Greenberg, David F.
1983 "Age and crime." Pp. 30–35 in Sanford H. Kadish (ed.), *Encyclopedia of Crime and Justice*. New York: Free Press.

Greenwood, Peter W.
1982   *Selective Incapacitation*. Santa Monica, CA: Rand.

Hammersley, Martyn and Paul Atkinson
1983   *Ethnography: Principles in Practice*. London: Tavistock Publications.

Hill, Percy H., H. A. Bedau, R. A. Chechile, W. J. Crochetiere
1979   *Making Decisions: A Multidisciplinary Introduction*. Reading, MA: Addison-Wesley.

Hirschi, Travis
1969   *Causes of Delinquency*. Berkeley: University of California Press.

Hirschi, Travis and Michael Gottfredson
1983   "Age and the explanation of crime." *American Journal of Sociology* 89: 552–84.

Holzman, Harold R.
1983   "The serious habitual property offender as moonlighter." *Journal of Criminal Law and Criminology* 73 (4): 1774–92.
1982   "Rationalistic opportunity perspective on criminal behavior: Toward a reformulation of the theoretical basis for the notion of property crime as work." *Crime and Delinquency* 28: 233–46.

Inciardi, James A.
1977   "In search of the class cannon: A field study of professional pickpockets." Pp. 55–77 in Robert S. Weppner (ed.), *Street Ethnography*. Beverly Hills, CA: Sage.

Innes, Christopher A.
1988   "Drug use and crime." Bureau of Justice Statistics Special Report (July): 1–8.

Irwin, John
1985   *The Jail*. Berkeley: The University of California Press.
1970   *The Felon*. Englewood Cliffs, NJ: Prentice-Hall.

Jacob, Herbert
1979   "Rationality and criminality." *Social Science Quarterly* 59: 584–85.

Jamieson, Katherine and Timothy J. Flanagan
1989   Sourcebook of Criminal Justice Statistics, 1988. Washington, DC: U.S. Department of Justice.

Jensen, Gary F.
1969   "Crime doesn't pay: Correlates of shared misunderstanding." *Social Problems* 17: 189–201.

Jensen, Gary F. and B. Grant Stitt
1982 "Words and misdeeds: Hypothetical choices versus past behavior as measure of deviance." Pp. 33–54 in John Hagan (ed.), *Deterrence Reconsidered*. Beverly Hills, CA: Sage.

Jensen, Gary F. and Maynard L. Erickson
1978 "The social meaning of sanctions." Pp. 119–36 in Marvin D. Krohn and Ronald L. Akers (eds.), *Crime, Law and Sanctions*. Beverly Hills, CA: Sage.

Jensen, Gary F., Maynard L. Erickson and Jack P. Gibbs
1978 "Perceived risk of punishment and self-reported delinquency." *Social Forces* 57: 57–78.

Johnson, Allen and Orna R. Johnson
1990 "Quality into quantity: On the measurement potential of ethnographic fieldnotes." Pp. 161–86 in Roger Sanjek (ed.), *Fieldnotes: The Makings of Anthropology*. Ithaca: Cornell University Press.

Johnson, Bruce
1991 "Drug control policies and strategies." Paper presented to the Academy of Criminal Justice Sciences, Nashville, TN, March.

Johnson, Eric and John Payne
1986 "The decision to commit a crime: An information-processing analysis." Pp. 170–85 in Derek B. Cornish and Ronald V. Clarke (eds.), *The Reasoning Criminal: Rational Choice Perspectives on Offending*. New York: Springer-Verlag.

Johnson, Robert
1981 *Condemned To Die: Life Under Sentence of Death*. Prospect Heights, IL: Waveland Press, Inc.

Kempf, Kimberly L.
1987 "Specialization and the criminal career." *Criminology* 25: 399–420.

Konecni, Vladimir and Ebbe B. Ebbesen
1979 "External validity of research in legal psychology." *Law and Human Behavior* 3: 39–70.

Konecni, Vladimir, Ebbe B. Ebbesen, and Daiva K. Konecni
1976 "Decision processes and risk taking in traffic: Driver responses to the onset of yellow light." *Journal of Applied Psychology* 6: 359–67.

Kramer, Ronald C.
1982 "From 'habitual offenders' to 'career criminals'." *Law and Human Behavior* 6: 273–93.

Lattimore, Pamela and Ann Witte
1986 "Models of decision-making under uncertainty: The criminal choice." Pp. 129–55 in Derek B. Cornish and Ronald V. Clarke (eds.), *The Reasoning Criminal*. New York: Springer-Verlag.

Lee, Wayne
1971 *Decision Theory and Human Behavior*. New York: John Wiley and Sons.

Letkemann, Peter
1973 *Crime as Work*. Englewood Cliffs, NJ: Prentice-Hall.

Lofland, John and Lyn H. Lofland
1984 *Analyzing Social Settings*. 2d ed. Belmont, CA: Wadsworth.

Lombroso, Cesare
1911 *Criminal Man*. Montclair, NJ: Patterson Smith.

Luckenbill, David F.
1985 "Entering male prostitution." *Urban Life* 14: 131–53.

Lundman, Richard J.
1986 "One-wave perceptual deterrence research: Some grounds for the renewed examination of cross-sectional methods." *Journal of Research in Crime and Delinquency* 23 (4): 370–88.

Maguire, Brendan
1988 "The applied dimension of radical criminology: A survey of prominent radical criminologists." *Sociological Spectrum* 8: 133–51.

Maguire, Mike
1980 "Burglary as occupation." *Home Office Research Bulletin* 10: 6–9.

Maguire, Mike and Trevor Bennett
1982 *Burglary in a Dwelling*. London: Heinemann.

Malcom X and Alex Haley
1964 *The Autobiography of Malcolm X*. New York: Grove Press.

Mann, Coramae R.
1984 *Female Crime and Delinquency*. Birmingham, AL: University of Alabama Press.

Martinson, Robert
1974 "What works? Questions and answers about prison reform." *Public Interest* 35 (Spring): 22–54.

McCarroll, Steve
1972 *Psychology Today*. 2d ed. Del Mar, CA: CRM Books.

McCracken, Grant
1988 *The Long Interview*. Beverly Hills, CA: Sage.

McPheters, Lee
1976 "Criminal behavior and the gains from crime." *Criminology* 14: 137–52.

Meier, Robert F.
1978 "The deterrence doctrine and public policy: A response to utilitarians." Pp. 233–47 in James A. Cramer (ed.), *Preventing Crime*. Beverly Hills, CA: Sage.

Meier, Robert and Weldon T. Johnson
1977 "Deterrence as social control: The legal and extra-legal production of conformity." *American Sociological Review* 42: 292–304.

Meisenhelder, Thomas N.
1977 "An exploratory study of exiting from criminal careers." *Criminology* 15: 319–34.

Menard, Scott and Delbert S. Elliott
1990 "Longitudinal and cross-sectional data collection and analysis in the study of crime and delinquency." *Justice Quarterly* 7 (1): 11–55.

Merton, Robert
1949 *Social Theory and Social Structure*. New York: The Free Press.

Minor, W. William
1978 "Deterrence research: Problems of theory and method." Pp. 21–45 in James A. Cramer (ed.), *Preventing Crime*. Beverly Hills, CA: Sage.

Minor, W. William and Joseph Harry
1982 "Deterrent and experiential effects in perceptual deterrence research: A replication and extension." *Journal of Research in Crime and Delinquency* 19: 190–203.

Morris, Allison
1987 *Women, Crime, and Criminal Justice*. Oxford, UK: Basil Blackwell.

Morris, Norval
1974 *The Future of Imprisonment*. Chicago: University of Chicago Press.
1951 *The Habitual Criminal*. Cambridge: Harvard University Press.

Morris, Norval and Gordon Hawkins
1970 *The Honest Politician's Guide to Crime Control*. Chicago: University of Chicago Press.

Nettler, Gwynn
1984 *Explaining Crime*. 3d ed. New York: McGraw-Hill.

Orsagh, Thomas
1983 "Is there a place for economics in criminology and criminal justice?" *Journal of Criminal Justice* 11 (5): 391–401.

Palmer, Jerry
1977 "Economic analyses of the deterrent effect of punishment: A review." *Journal of Research in Crime and Delinquency* 14: 4–21.

Parker, Jerry and Harold Grasmick
1979 "Linking actual and perceived certainty of punishment." *Criminology* 17: 366–79.

Paternoster, Raymond
1987 "The deterrent effect of the perceived certainty and severity of punishment: A review of the evidence and issues." *Justice Quarterly* 4: 173–217.

Paternoster, R., L.E. Saltzman, T.G. Chiricos, and G.P. Waldo
1985 "Assessments of risk and behavioral experience: An exploratory study of change." *Criminology* 23: 417–36.
1983 "Perceived risk and social control: Do sanctions really deter?" *Law & Society Review* 17 (3): 457–79.
1982a "Perceived risk and deterrence: Methodological artifacts in perceptual deterrence research." *Journal of Criminal Law and Criminology* 73: 1238–58.
1982b "Causal ordering in deterrence research." Pp. 55–70 in John Hagan (ed.), *Deterrence Reconsidered*. Beverly Hills, CA: Sage.

Patton, Michael Q.
1987 *How to Use Qualitative Methods in Evaluation*. Beverly Hills, CA: Sage.

Petersilia, Joan
1980 "Criminal career research: A review of recent evidence." Pp. 321–79 in Norval Morris and Michael Tonry (eds.), *Crime and Justice: An Annual Review of Research*, Vol. 2. Chicago: University of Chicago Press.

Petersilia, Joan, Peter Greenwood and Marvin Lavin
1978 *Criminal Careers of Habitual Felons*. Washington, DC: U.S. Department of Justice.

Peterson, Mark A., Harriet B. Braiker, and Suzanne M. Polich
1980 *Doing Crime: A Survey of California Prison Inmates*. Santa Monica, CA: Rand.

Physician's Desk Reference
1977 *Physician's Desk Reference*. Oradell, NJ: Medican Economics Company.

Piliavin, Irving, C. Thornton, R. Gartner, and R.L. Matusuda
1986   "Crime, deterrence and rational choice." *American Sociological Review* 51: 101-19.
Rankin, Joseph H. and L. Edward Wells
1983   "The social context of deterrence." *Sociology and Social Research* 67: 18-39.
Reiman, Jeffrey
1990   *The Rich get Richer and the Poor get Prison*. 3d ed. New York: Macmillan.
Rengert, George and John Wasilchick
1985   *Suburban Burglary*. Springfield, IL: Charles C. Thomas.
Reppetto, T. A.
1974   *Residential Crime*. Cambridge, MA: Ballinger.
Rettig, S. and H. E. Rawson
1963   "The risk hypothesis in predictive judgments of unethical behavior." *Journal of Abnormal and Social Psychology* 66: 243-48.
Richards, Pamela and Charles R. Tittle
1982   "Socioeconomic status and perceptions of personal arrest probabilities." *Criminology* 20: 329-46.
Roebuck, Julian B.
1967   *Criminal Typology*. Springfield, IL: Charles C. Thomas.
Ross, H. Laurence
1973   "Law, science and accidents: The British Safety Act of 1967." *Journal of Legal Studies* 2: 1-78.
1975   "The Scandinavian myth: The effectiveness of drinking-and-driving legislation in Sweden and Norway." *Journal of Legal Studies* 4: 285-98.
1982   "Interrupted time series of deterrence of drinking and driving." Pp. 71-97 in John Hagan (ed.), *Deterrence Reconsidered*. Beverly Hills, CA: Sage.
Rowe, David C., D. Wayne Osgood, and W. Alan Nicewander
1990   "A latent trait approach to unifying criminal careers." *Criminology* 28: 237-70.
Saltzman, Linda, R. Paternoster, G.P. Waldo, and T.G. Chiricos
1982   "Deterrence and experiential effects: The problem of causal order in perceptual deterrence research." *Journal of Research in Crime and Delinquency* 19: 172-89.
Sanjek, Roger
1990   "On ethnographic validity." Pp. 385-418 in *Fieldnotes: The Makings of Anthropology*. Ithaca, NY: Cornell University Press.

Scull, Andrew T.
1984   *Decarceration.* 2d ed. New Brunswick, NJ: Rutgers University Press.

Schwartz, B.
1968   "The effect in Philadelphia of Pennsylvania's increased penalties for rape and attempted rape." *Journal of Criminal Law and Criminology* 59: 509–15.

Shaw, Clifford R.
1966   *The Jack Roller: A Delinquent Boy's Own Story.* Chicago: University of Chicago Press.

Shaw, Clifford R. and Henry D. McKay
1938   *Brothers in Crime.* Chicago: University of Chicago Press.

Shover, Neal
1985   *Aging Criminals.* Beverly Hills, CA: Sage.
1973   "The social organization of burglary." *Social Problems* 20: 499–514.
1972   "Structures and careers in burglary." *Journal of Criminal Law, Criminology and Police Science* 63: 540–49.

Silberman, Matthew
1976   "Toward a theory of criminal deterrence." *American Sociological Review* 41: 442–61.

Sills, David L.
1968   *International Encyclopedia of the Social Sciences.* New York: Free Press.

Simon, H.A.
1976   *Administrative Behavior.* New York: Free Press.

Sjoberg, Lennart
1987   "Risk, power and rationality." Pp. 239–43 in Lennart Sjoberg (ed.), *Risk and Society.* London: Allen and Unwin.

Sjoquist, David L.
1973   "Property crime and economic behavior: Some empirical results." *American Economic Review* 63 (June): 439–46.

Spradley, James P.
1979   *The Ethnographic Interview.* New York: Holt, Rinehart and Winston.

Sullivan, Richard F.
1973   "The economics of crime: An introduction to the literature." *Crime and Delinquency* 19: 138–49.

Sutherland, Edwin H.
1937   *The Professional Thief.* Chicago: The University of Chicago Press.

Sutherland, Edwin H. and Donald R. Cressey
1978 *Criminology.* 10th ed. Philadelphia: J.B. Lippincott Company.
Sykes, Gresham M. and David Matza
1957 "Techniques of neutralization: A theory of delinquency." *American Sociological Review* 22: 664–70.
Terkel, Studs
1972 *Working.* New York: Avon Books.
Theodorson, George A. and Achilles G. Theodorson
1969 *A Modern Dictionary of Sociology.* New York: Barnes & Noble.
Tillman, Robert
1987 "The size of the criminal population: The prevalence and incidence of adult arrest." *Criminology* 25: 561–79.
Tittle, Charles R.
1980 *Sanctions and Social Deviance: The Question of Deterrence.* New York: Praeger.
1977 "Sanction fear and the maintenance of social order." *Social Forces* 55 (March): 579–96.
1969 "Crime rates and legal sanctions." *Social Problems* 16: 408–23.
Tittle, Charles R. and Alan R. Rowe
1977 "Life cycle changes and criminal propensity." *Sociological Quarterly* 18: 223–36.
Toby, Jackson
1964 "Is punishment necessary?" *Journal of Criminal Law, Criminology and Police Science* 55: 332–37.
Trebach, Arnold S.
1987 *The Great Drug War.* New York: Macmillan.
Tuck, Mary and David Riley
1986 "The theory of reasoned action: A decision theory of crime." Pp. 156–69 in Derek B. Cornish and Ronald V. Clarke (eds.), *The Reasoning Criminal.* New York: Springer-Verlag.
Tullock, George
1974 "Does punishment deter crime?" *The Public Interest* 36: 103–11.
Tunnell, Kenneth D.
1990a "Film at eleven: Fetishism and the commodification of crime." Paper presented at the Academy of Criminal Justice Sciences, Denver, CO, March.

1990b   "Property criminals as the lumpen proletariat: A serendipitous finding." *Nature, Society, and Thought* 3: 39–55.

Tversky, Amos and Daniel Kahneman
1982   "Availability: A heuristic for judging frequency and probability." Pp. 163–78 in Daniel Kahneman, Paul Slovic and Amos Tversky (eds.), *Judgement Under Uncertainty: Heuristics and Biases*. Cambridge: Cambridge University Press.
1981   "The framing of decisions and the psychology of choice." *Science* 211: 453–58.
1974   "Judgment under uncertainty: Heuristics and biases." *Science* 185: 1124–31.

Uniform Crime Reports
1989   *Crime in the United States, 1988*. Washington, DC: U.S. Department of Justice.
1988   *Crime in the United States, 1987*. Washington, DC: U.S. Department of Justice.
1986   *Crime in the United States, 1985*. Washington, DC: U.S. Department of Justice.

United States Department of Justice
1983   *Report to the Nation on Crime and Justice*. Washington, DC: U.S. Government Printing Office.

United States Department of Labor
1988   *Employment and Training Report of the President*. Washington, DC: Government Printing Office.

Van Doren, Bob
1972   *Psychology Today*. 2d ed. Del Mar, CA: CRM Books.

Visher, Christy A.
1986   "The Rand inmate survey: A reanalysis" Pp. 161–211 in Alfred Blumstein, Jacqueline Cohen, Jeffrey A. Roth, and Christy A. Visher (eds.), *Criminal Careers and "Career Criminals,"* Vol. 2. Washington, DC: National Academy Press.

Waldo, Gordon P. and Theodore Chiricos
1972   "Perceived penal sanction and self-reported criminality: A neglected approach to deterrence research." *Social Problems* 19: 522–40.

Walker, Samuel
1985   *Sense and Nonsense about Crime*. Monterey, CA: Brooks/Cole.

Wallace, Don and Drew Humphries
1981   "Urban crime and capitalist accumulation: 1950–1971." Pp. 140–56 in David F. Greenberg (ed.), *Crime and Capitalism*. Palo Alto, CA: Mayfield.

Walsh, Dermot
1986 *Heavy Business: Commercial Burglary and Robbery*. London: Routledge and Kegan Paul.
Walters, Glenn D.
1990 *The Criminal Lifestyle*. Beverly Hills, CA: Sage.
Weber, Max
1968 *Economy and Society*. Guenther Roth and Claus Wittich (eds.). Translated by Ephraim Fischoff from the original edition (1956). New York: Bedminster.
Wilson, James Q. and Richard J. Herrnstein
1985 *Crime and Human Nature*. New York: Simon and Schuster.
Wilson, William J.
1987 *The Truly Disadvantaged: The Inner City, the Underclass and Public Policy*. Chicago: University of Chicago Press.
Wright, Eric O.
1973 *The Politics of Punishment: A Critical Analysis of Prisons in America*. New York: Harper & Row.
Wright, Kevin N.
1985 *The Great American Crime Myth*. New York: Praeger.
Zimring, Franklin E.
1977 "Punishment and deterrence: Bad checks in Nebraska—a study in complex threats." Pp. 173-89 in David F. Greenberg (ed.), *Corrections and Punishment*. Beverly Hills, CA: Sage.
1973 *Deterrence: The Legal Threat in Crime Control*. Chicago: University of Chicago Press.
1972 "Of doctors, deterrence, and the dark figure of crime: A note on abortion in Hawaii." *University of Chicago Law Review* 39: 699-721.
1971 *Perspective on deterrence*. Washington, DC: National Health Service Publication.